AF587616

Darkness Retreat

An Exciting Journey to the Source of Being

With 30 personal accounts from participants over the past 5 years.

By Bharati Corinna and Martin Glanert

1st Edition (2018)

Editors: Bharati Corinna Glanert und Martin Glanert
Schönbüchstr. 24
77887 Sasbachwalden
Germany

www.spiritbalance.com
www.darknessretreat.net

Authors: Bharati Corinna Glanert and Martin Glanert
Design, Illustration: Hannah Albrecht and Marcus Herrmann
Translation: Christi Chambers Dufour
Cover photo: www.fotolia.com

Publishing House: tao.de in Kamphausen Media GmbH,
Bielefeld, www.tao.de, email: info@tao.de

Bibliographic information of the German National Library:
The German National Library lists this publication in the
German National Library; detailed bibliographic data
are available on the Internet at http://dnb.d-nb.de.

ISBN Paperback: 978-3-96240-174-0
ISBN e-Book: 978-3-96240-176-4

Table of Contents

My Path to the Darkness Retreat

Preface from Bharati Corinna Glanert

I spent many years of my life in India where I came into contact with powerful yogis and sadhus. It was a time full of inspiration and openings to new worlds where I learned countless spiritual practices and energetic processes. After years of practicing specific and intensive meditation techniques, I experienced a strong awakening and deep insight to very high levels of consciousness. These years of completely stepping away from the western world revealed to me that conditions to achieve true enlightenment are available to every soul! I am deeply grateful for having experienced this very precious time.

In India, I also learned about spiritual practices taking place in the dark. Although I found it highly fascinating, during this time in my life other techniques were at the forefront. So it was only when I had arrived back in Germany in 2010, that I did my first Darkness Retreat.

My first Darkness Retreat was a very powerful experience that touched me deeply and showed me what my mission is here on earth. My time in the darkness was spent completely alone, without any spiritual counselling or guidance. This was far from easy and it was then I realized that for many people, a Darkness Retreat would be even more effective if accompanied by competent spiritual counselling. This would create a safe space for people to completely trust and let go. I knew that in this type of setting and with my knowledge from India, it would be possible for me to consciously guide and introduce these deep experiences.

After my retreat, I started to bring my vision into the world and since 2011, I have been successfully leading supervised Darkness Retreats in different countries. The project has grown to the point that requires training more people in this method of Darkness Retreat facilitation and now, I'm supported with a full team of counsellors here at Spiritbalance.

It is my heartfelt desire to help people in their quest for true spiritual growth. Connecting with higher souls, astral travel and out-of-body projection, darshans and other similar experiences are often very healing, consciousness-expanding and helpful experiences for personal development. For me, the Darkness Retreat is the absolute royal path.

For more than 17 years, my dedication to researching spirituality and extra-sensory perception has given me many techniques and ways to consciously invoke spiritual experiences. They are all very powerful and intense, yet in my opinion, it is through Darkness Retreats that one is able to experience the fastest and strongest effects.

For many, it's a catalyst - a fast track -for true spiritual development.

This book is a collection of personal experiences from our guests and provides insight into the possibilities a Darkness Retreat can offer.

I'm very happy that so many of our previous retreat participants opened up to write about all of their different experiences for this book. You will see how unique the Darkness Retreat is and how it is working for each individual.

May this book support and help you find your own path to grow and experience deep healing.

With lightful greetings,

Bharati Corinna Glanert

My Path to the Darkness Retreat

Preface from Martin Glanert

In 2011 when I met my future wife on a trip to India, little did I know how far we would travel together on our future life path. I didn't know that we would raise two wonderful children together, nor did I know that the Darkness Retreat would be such a powerful technique for my own self-discovery and personal development.

I must admit, in the beginning I was very skeptical about the whole idea of a Darkness Retreat. I couldn't imagine isolation in darkness could really have a lasting effect on the participant's life and personality. But it was not long after that I was proven wrong. Certainly, it was a big advantage for me to be able to experience the many Darkness Retreats in our seminar center, without being directly involved. I have a very strong, empirical education in psychology and behavioral sciences, and my years studying at university left their mark. More often than not, I considered that truth could be proven only by empirical and verifiable methods. But over the course of time, I witnessed how some of the Darkness Retreat participants had wonderful, as well as extreme, experiences and how they left the special retreat as a changed person.

Over time, I realized that darkness is simply a catalyst for certain inner processes: physical, mental and energetic. Bharati began asking for my help in certain situations and urged me more and more to become actively involved in the counselling and take over the daily conversations. So I slowly, but surely, took on the role of a counsellor. If this progression had not been so organic or if had I approached it more cautiously, my mind would have definitely rebelled. The experiences that many participants had during the Darkness Retreat were just too extraordinary to deny. Sometimes their experiences were so extreme that they only dared to share them with us, and no one else. Otherwise, they thought they would have been declared crazy. Over time my perception and thinking changed. I realized that a distinct separation between body, mind and soul doesn't exist and that these are only auxiliary constructions of the unconscious mind to explain reality to us. A reality that is mostly perceived visually. As soon as this channel gets switched off during the Darkness Retreat, all the concepts we normally use to explain our reality lose their importance.

In 2013 it was time. I went into the darkness to experience it for myself. After sleeping deeply and soundly for a long time, my sleep, dreams and reality quickly became intertwined. After my thoughts had calmed down, the experiences began. I felt I was simultaneously in two places: in the darkness of my room and also at another place in my dreams. I slept yet I was also awake. I dreamed, but at the same time I experienced things that were more real than reality. I had the sensation that I flew across vast fields. After a while I heard my inner voice speak to me. I had always assumed that this would be a sacred and holy moment, accompanied by a drum roll or a string quartet. The voice was not really a voice, but more a confirmation. Not like words one simply writes on paper, but more like a memory of something I had read. My inner self had spoken to me and gave me very concrete instructions with regard to my future behavior. For example, I should walk barefoot to become more connected to the earth.

During my clinical psychologist training at university, I did an internship lasting several months with one of my professors where we treated patients according to the prescribed guidelines. Although cognitive behavioral therapy is the standard method in today's world, my professor's approach was more psychodynamically oriented. I still remember a situation that happened during a patient's first meeting. My professor explained to me that in order to have a better understanding of the internal dynamics behind the patient's façade, it was his explicit intention not to have a fixed framework for the meeting. He believed that when a fixed framework is used, the patient's response is only according to this structure. If we really want understand what is going on for the person, then the interaction with them must be free of any structures.

In contrast to many other methods for gaining inner knowledge, the Darkness Retreat has a big advantage. It is the dissolution of structure. After a period of time without external and internal structure, our deep inner structure appears automatically. It doesn't matter if we refer to it as our personality, soul, or whatever. Additionally, through the absence of external stimuli, our awareness searches for new information. Witnessing the unfolding of our inner mysteries seems almost like watching a play with many scenes or a concert with several movements. Sometimes it passes quickly and sometimes slowly, sometimes with happiness and sometimes with sadness. And here, as in a concert, there are always motifs that return and reveal the essence of oneself. And it is this essence of our true self that reveals itself before our inner eyes.

With love and gratitude,

Martin Glanert

The Tao says:

"When you go into the dark and this becomes total, the darkness soon turns into light."

Mantak Chia

Darkness Retreat

Going Back into Darkness

All of us have already experienced a long and intensive Darkness Retreat at least once - while being nurtured in our mother's warm and comforting womb. During this first experience, we were in absolute union with our mother for nine months, peacefully merged with the universe. A Darkness Retreat is often like a conscious return to this primal experience where we not only receive new knowledge, but also reawaken our own soul, with all its wisdom and spiritual strength.

Using darkness as a tool for sensory deprivation and deconditioning is a self-discovery method that belongs to the teachings of many ancient cultures and religions. In the pre-Buddhist Bon religion of Tibet, the Darkness Retreat has already been described as the "Golden Path to Enlightenment" and is also known to the indigenous peoples of South America. For example, kivas are underground, circular ceremonial and meeting rooms of Pueblo cultures. Even Pythagoras built an underground chamber below his house in southern Italy, where he spent long periods of time in conscious retreat.

In order to trigger these intensive, deep energetic processes during a retreat, it is important that the area of the Darkness Retreat, including the bathroom, hallways and corridor, is completely blacked out. Only with these conditions during the entire retreat period, can we become completely free from optical stimuli and become open to the profound processes that darkness offers us.

The longer one stays in a protected location in total darkness, the more intense the spiritual experiences will be. Darkness itself becomes a guru. The Sanskrit word "Gu" means darkness or ignorance, "Ru" denotes the remover of this darkness. Therefore, someone who removes the darkness and ignorance from us, is a guru. And this is exactly what darkness will do. When we are ready, it can lead us to the Divine light. Darkness is a primal force that helps us to grow personally and spiritually. When we can go into it for an extended period of time, we experience deep healing within ourselves, our being and our strengths.

An extended stay in darkness is also called "Darkness Therapy", as it is extremely healing on many levels to be by oneself for a period of time without distractions. In contrast to modern therapy practices, Darkness Therapy doesn't work with individual problems. It unifies and works on the whole being. Overall, it is about the connection with ourselves and with the universe. To feel union. When we are in deep connection with our soul, we often experience amazing things about our existence and ourselves. Under these circumstances, the mind will naturally slip into a meditative state. It then becomes easy to use mantras to develop and expand this meditative energy. Far away from any external stimuli, the Darkness Retreat allows us to begin exploring our inner life in a very natural way. At first, when the mind no longer has any external objects at its disposal, it will often find and offer a full range of interesting ideas and suggestions for us to deal with. Observing our mind during the first phases in darkness is an intense, insightful process that reveals much about individual patterns and conditioning.

After a few days in the dark, the mind becomes calm and the attention gradually moves inward. Many participants experience wonderful feelings of unity and deep inner peace which fill and carry the heart and spirit.

Everything that we have ever experienced becomes stored as information on the cellular and energetic levels in our body. When the outside light is extinguished, our inner light appears and illuminates these buried areas of our being. The external darkness paves the way to the inner light and opens the space for profound, positive changes.

As this first view becomes directed on our inner life, it's possible that all the unprocessed themes from the past that have been waiting for such a long time to finally be processed and let go, will appear. All of a sudden, those suppressed feelings and painful injuries from the past that have been buried deep within our subconscious and out of view in our everyday awareness, now have space to be observed and transformed.

Stillness as a Way to the True Self

The outer world never rests. It is in constant turmoil. We all know this. Flickering TVs, blasting stereos, ringing smartphones, ubiquitous internet and radiating satellites - the world around us becomes continually louder. The human brain has to sort through and process the constant noise, images and impressions. Unless the brain takes a break from this constant inundation, people become unfocused with very low energy. In today's fast-paced world, it is absolutely essential to take time for a complete withdrawal so our system is not put under continuous stress by constant over-stimulation.

A very effective method to balance these processing mechanisms is a retreat in a completely darkened space. Far away from any external sources of light, we can immediately begin an inner journey. Our view is automatically directed inwards and it quickly becomes obvious how important stillness is for the regeneration of our own health.

It's only when this constant inundation of stimulus stops for a longer period of time that the brain gets a well-deserved break. This allows a recovery phase for our mental capacity and resources, as well as normalizing the blood pressure.

Within the brain there is a resting network known as the default mode network (DMN). This particular network of the brain becomes activated only when there is no new information to process and no tasks to undertake. This makes it much easier to observe and reflect on ourselves when we are in retreat and resting.

Often in this inner space, we connect and get in touch with our memories from the past. All that is revealed brings a higher and more meaningful understanding. Transformational processes get a big boost with the help of darkness. These life-changing experiences in the silence of a Darkness Retreat often lead to profound emotional and psychological healing. Some guests report an extraordinary deep relaxation which they have only been able to experience in the silence of the dark.

Sometimes it can be that the silence is unbearable. All themes need to be looked at before they can disappear, which is not always pleasant. In these phases, it's important to remember that it is exactly these experiences where healing is happening on the deepest levels. Old injuries can be healed and new perspectives can be integrated. This new sense of inner freedom allows us to grow and fulfill our greatest potential as humans. It forms the basis of creating a positive and peaceful future for ourselves and with others.

Intensive Spiritual Experiences

A retreat into total darkness is so powerful due to the visual channel being completely switched off. This removes the greatest source of distraction for our consciousness and shortly thereafter, an expansion of awareness happens on its own.

After a while, the other senses are automatically sharpened and refined. The third eye opens and it becomes possible to have visions, clairvoyant experiences and encounters with other dimensions. Also happening, either consciously or unconsciously, is the internal monologue with the soul and subconscious mind.

With no external stimuli, the inner voice becomes amplified as it is also connected with the soul. This happens through receiving flashes of insight, unique truths and wisdom. Our inner knowing is suddenly and completely clear. Making decisions is easy. One's own path is clearly revealed. Answers to important life questions arrive to us spontaneously. Deep mental rest sets in.

Contact with spirit beings, the deceased and the primal light of one's own soul all become possible.

During the Darkness Retreat, each participant goes through it in their own way having spiritual experiences through the different possibilities that arise. It is often felt as a deep self-awareness, an inner contemplation and observation of mental processes.

The most frequent perception occurring in the Darkness Retreat are light apparitions. After some time in the dark, the internal light becomes physically visible. This is a deeply transformative experience. In this context, the word "enlightenment" takes on a completely new meaning. Out-of-body projections are also frequently mentioned, as are encounters with loved ones, the deceased, angels and ascended spirits. The access to spiritual worlds becomes wide open and provides the consciousness with a long-lasting expansion.

As we manage to let go of our surroundings, we stop projecting ourselves onto the outside world and literally begin to look within. Through this, it is possible to transform the Ego-Experience into simply 'being', which brings with it a wonderful sense of unity and 'having arrived'.

Different Levels of Spiritual Phenomena

As we begin to go deeper into our spirituality, we see that these intensive experiences are constructed on a multi-level, step-by-step process.

First we see rays of light, or our individual soul light, glowing in the dark. This is a light that never goes out and penetrates through everything. This first stage is usually accompanied by confusion or not knowing what to feel.

On the second level, we start to feel and see more. For example, three-dimensional yantras become visible.

At the third level, it becomes possible to communicate and have direct, physical contact with high spirit beings.

Spontaneous Out-of-Body Experiences

The astral plane is most frequently accessed by people who have a lot of experience with meditation. But from time to time, beginners also report about astral travel and similar experiences. The intensity of this experience can be overwhelming and raises a lot of new questions for oneself, the way we perceive the world and fundamental questions about death and impermanence.

A Darkness Retreat is not the only way to astral travel, but the phases of long and dark meditation open up this incredible potential easily. Years of extensive research in the field of out-of-body experiences and astral travel has proven that these highly energetic spiritual experiences can happen to everyone.

Out-of-body projection normally occurs when the body is in a state of complete relaxation. There are many people who experience this particular phenomenon of feeling "out-of-body" several times in their life, and usually in very spontaneous ways and situations.

Spontaneous, out-of-body experiences often occur during near-death experiences, such as serious accidents. Sometimes women experience this while giving birth. In all transcendent experiences it can happen that the soul detaches itself from the physical body and the person suddenly becomes conscious of seeing their own body from being outside of it. This type of transcendent experience can happen spontaneously in a Darkness Retreat.

Consciously Creating Out-of-Body Experiences

All of us have daily out-of-body experiences on an unconscious level - while sleeping at night. Yet only a few people remember them when they are awake. It is, however, possible to induce conscious astral travel with very specific and concrete techniques. Those who use these easy-to-learn exercises can consistently achieve amazing results relatively quickly.

Some of the retreat guests took advantage of the darkness to practice these techniques and were able to produce at will and relatively easily, out-of-body projection. With conscious and deliberate intention, they were able to successfully switch over and access the high vibrational astral plane. Such impressionable soul experiences are an absolute enrichment for one's own life and self-understanding. This process is particularly well-supported in darkness.

Those who have learned to intentionally access the astral plane never forget these high vibrational experiences after returning to body consciousness. On these levels, high energetic encounters become possible. The increase and expansion of our sensory perception can also result in clairaudience and clairvoyance. On the astral plane there are no physical limitations, the blind and paralyzed can see and move. For these people, such miraculous occurrences bring profound healing. We are able to heal so much of our pain and negativity that we hold inside by understanding who we truly are. Opening up to our fear of dying can change our entire self-belief by realizing it is actually a wonderful, unifying experience. The desire becomes stronger to get to the bottom of essential questions and understand the meaning of our life on earth.

Clairvoyant and Clairaudient Experiences

Clairvoyance and clairaudience can happen in the Darkness Retreat even without reaching the level of the astral plane. It's often the case that these qualities and special abilities remain even after the Darkness Retreat. Whether we can maintain them depends on our lifestyle. The more we care for these gifts, use them consciously and practice them intensively with a consistent spiritual practice, it becomes easier for us to reach that high level once again.

There is a vast range of spiritual experiences to discover and this becomes accelerated by the physical process of being in the dark. If we are in complete darkness for days, the biochemistry of the human brain changes enormously and starts to put spiritual experiences in motion.

The Body's Own Biochemical Process

Extrasensory abilities are directly related to the pineal gland, a pea-sized, pinecone-shaped hormone gland in the middle of our brain. It controls the internal clock, regulates sleep, the aging process and is responsible for our intuition. From a spiritual point of view, it is the soul's headquarters and the gate between the physical and the subtle worlds.

Within the first three days in complete darkness, the pineal gland starts to produce and secrete enough melatonin, the hormone that helps regulate biological rhythms, for the brainwave frequency to reach theta frequency. The frequency of theta waves lie in the range between 3 and 8 Hz and is predominant during relaxation, meditation and deep trance states. They are waves that send signals to and from the unconscious mind. So it's not surprising that many Darkness Retreat participants feel an increased need for rest and sleep in the first few days. In Theta State, people have access to their unconscious mind, to suppressed feelings, to personal stories, as well as to their creative potential and an increased ability to focus and concentrate. During this phase, lucid dreams and insightful visions can occur. The mind becomes clear and the Darkness Retreat participant can gradually build up their connection with Divine Consciousness. During this phase, it can also happen that existing symptoms worsen before healing.

In the following days there is often an activation of the third eye. As soon as the secretion of melatonin has settled to a level of 15 - 20 mg, the pineal gland can start producing the superconductor, Pinoline. The brain maintains the frequency where the neurotransmitter production is stimulated by the epiphysis. The epiphysis, in turn, is responsible for converting the melatonin into DMT, which stimulates the third eye. Under normal circumstances, Pinoline is secreted only in a mother's body during birth or during near-death experiences. It strengthens lucid dreams and stimulates the body's healing powers. It's also possible that clairvoyance, clairaudience and apparitions of light occur. One can intuitively grasp the meaning of existence, as well as the "order of all things". The pineal gland serves as a receiving channel for our soul and allows us to access information from other planes of consciousness.

After approximately six to eight days in the Darkness Retreat, the pineal gland can produce the neurohormone 5-MeO-DMT, which is also called Akashon. This molecule activates another 40 percent of the cerebral cortex and stimulates the nervous system to become increasingly self-aware. There is an infinite expansion of the emotional body. In this state, the darkness gives way to a bright light and a feeling of rebirth flows through the person. Profound feelings of unity with the universe, empathy and astral projections triggered by the bright light are not a rarity during this phase.

Between the ninth and twelfth day in the Darkness Retreat, the DMT level can rise up to 25mg. DMT is the activating neurotransmitter for the pineal gland, directly related to the third eye. Strong visual experiences can happen. After some time, one can begin to see the infrared and ultraviolet light range and perceive heat patterns emanating from objects and entities in the room. There is also the possibility during this phase for the energy body to travel beyond space and time and have extremely high vibrational and intense experiences. The veil of illusion is lifted and unity to the source of our being is revealed. Transcendental experiences and feelings of unconditional love become increasingly present.

The Journey to Deep Inner Peace

In today's world we are primarily influenced through the visual channel. Most information from our surroundings comes through our eyes. Even if we're not paying close attention to these specific sensory impressions, these images reach our subconscious, form beliefs and influence our thinking and actions. All day long we are guided, whether we like it or not, by the temptations we receive through our senses.

Our vision is an important tool to help us find the way through our complex environment and navigate through everyday life, yet all too often the entire flood of information leads to powerful unconscious identifications, prejudices, harmful beliefs, etc. Ultimately, we forget that our mind's constant activity stops us from getting in touch with ourselves and our surroundings.

Many people who meditate regularly are able to reach a state of mind that is balanced and not distracted by the stimuli of the outside world. However, anyone who has meditated already knows what a challenge it is to simply meditate all the external stimulus away. It's easier to switch off the outside stimuli, which happens completely and automatically in a Darkness Retreat. After a few days in total darkness our system switches to night mode.

The deep relaxation is so huge that some guests report having never felt so relaxed in their entire life.

A Darkness Retreat is like traveling on the express train to deep inner peace - it actually is a real alternative to a relaxing holiday! A complete withdrawal of stimuli acts as a catalyst for relaxation. The regeneration that comes from letting go on all levels and being in a place to maintain it happens very quickly. Darkness is a magical, primal force that helps us with personal and spiritual development. The more time we are able to give ourselves for this process, the more we are able to experience deep inner healing.

Personal Experience as Holistic Healing

The longer the participants remain in the dark, the more layers of the being can be penetrated. From conditioned identities as mother, father, child, friend, foe, teacher, helper, businessperson, winner or loser until we reach the innermost self. The soul is a part of our divine origin: it is eternal, full of wisdom and full of bliss. The soul was never born and the soul will never pass away. The soul does not suffer, it is perfect and always connected to our spirit. When we feel pain, then it's either the body, the emotions or the mind that suffers, but never the soul. The soul is always truthful. It is pure and free from any pain.

If it happens that our soul-light appears within the framework of a Darkness Retreat, this is an indication that we are undergoing a deep, extremely healing transformation and experiencing positive changes in ourselves and our perception of the world. An experience like this gives people balance and confidence for their projects. Feeling strengthened, this indescribable and beautiful experience leaves a profound impression and helps many Darkness Retreat guests continue through life feeling more relaxed and at ease.

Darkness Retreat

Experiences from our Guests

Kai from Nuremberg, Germany, Age 48

First retreat in January 2012 for 14 days
Second retreat in March-April 2016 for 36 days

Since my youth I've been practicing meditation. The first book I read on the subject was the classic text, "Hara, the Vital Center of Man". I then continued with Patanjali. It was my fascination with shamanism that finally brought me to the Darkness Retreat. Among shamans and ancient druids, there is a ritual of retreating into caves. A highlight of this experience was my retreat in the cave of Wendelstein, Imbolc, in 2008. The temperature was 4 ° Celsius and the retreat lasted 8 days long. My experience in yoga helped me to endure the rather chilly climate. It was a great experience.

During the first retreat, my idea and wish was to broaden my experience by accessing other planes of existence. For the second retreat, my focus was to meet Hanuman. My fears were very minimal about attracting any negative forces.

On the first Darkness Retreat, I had already prepared by switching to a vegetarian diet. For the second retreat, I prepared by reciting the Hanuman Mantra and Hanuman Chalisa.

I experienced so many things during the Darkness Retreat. In the first retreat I had a light out-of-body projection. Although there was no light, my shadow appeared on the wall. An angel showed me what bliss is and that it is waiting for me once I am completely rid of my physical shell. There was a symbol that appeared as a door gap. I could peer through it and feel that something was there. It was absolutely real! I had an encounter with a picture of Jesus holding a lamb in his right arm and a cross in the left arm with a halo over his head. The following day while in deep meditation, he spoke and instructed me to keep letting go. I didn't know anymore what to do or whether I should meditate at all. Then he told me I should also let go of that concern. When I was able to just sit, all of my thoughts emptied and I had a Satori experience. In Zen, one doesn't directly aim to achieve this state but rather "waits" until it occurs spontaneously. Once I had a Kundalini experience with warming, sweating, etc. and then a few moments afterward, I received a great blessing. It was an embrace from Durga, the Divine Mother, whom I had not focused on at all. Another great darshan came on about the 10th day. I didn't know anything about darshan or the meaning in Sanskrit, but there before me, a yogi appeared, like a film negative. Then I heard the Light Mantra and there, sat a man in a white robe. I didn't know him but I really loved listening to the mantra. I didn't know why but I just really liked it. It made me feel very good. Later I learned that this was a great blessing from Swami Ramalinga. This ascended yogi, who reached samadhi enlightenment, had come to visit me.

Then, during my second retreat, I was very surprised to hear "my" beautiful light mantra again. On the second day there was a power failure and in the right corner of the room stood Hanuman. It really didn't fit at all into my concept of a "Darkness Retreat" and at first it was so overwhelming, until I could eventually figure it out and make some sense of it. I thought that there was absolutely no way that an experience like this could happen so fast! He had obviously shown up to teach me a lesson. I also heard angels and light beings talking but didn't see them. Everything started happening so quickly. An Angel, a Deva and a Spirit sat on my bed and even though I had no idea what it was, I felt it to be absolutely positive. Once someone held my hand. It felt like someone familiar that I'd known for a long time. At some point, I asked for things to appear more discreetly because I could no longer sleep. Then everything disappeared. Later on during the Hanuman Sadhana, Hanuman appeared and told me my mission in life.

During my first retreat, I felt very balanced and happy. In the second retreat, I had mixed feelings because at that time three people in my family were ill. But I always received beautiful signs, both secular and non-secular, which gradually calmed me down. In the end I was glad to know that everything would get better. And due to everything that happened, there was a point where I couldn't wait to go home.

For me personally, the Darkness Retreat gave me a confirmation that I'm doing the right things in my life, that it's truly necessary and I'm not just chasing after pipe dreams. It helped me to forgive both myself and other people. My perspective to observe expanded and I have certainly become more wise, yet also more spontaneous. The internal process which I went through during the days in the Darkness Retreat ranged from curiosity, inner peace, small worries (what if scenarios...) to joy, harmony, inner strength, more self-determination and letting go to accept whatever may come.

The moment I "went back to the light", I felt as though I was diving into a new world with very different eyes. I also learned not to hold on to these higher experiences but rather, integrate them.

After the Darkness Retreat, I've been able to take things more lightly and let go of everything that happens both internally and externally in my life. Whether it's good or not so good, I let it run its course from one direction to the other and then bring it back onto the right track. Why should I be that mouse in the drum that, after every beat, goes running left and right to the other side? Even if Mount Meru started shaking, my basic trust is firmly grounded in the wisdom of Divine order. Also since then, my spiritual chakras and their link to the communication of my higher self with the Divine Spirit is working really well.

I recommend the Darkness Retreat to all those who are on a path of self-discovery, regardless which type. All themes that bind us can be looked at and resolved. At this time I'm not sure if I'll do another Darkness Retreat. Maybe it will happen at some point, just spontaneously.

Martin from Stuttgart, Germany, Age 35

10-Day Individual Retreat in March - April 2013

My name is Martin. I'm 35 and a writer and entrepreneur from Stuttgart. Being well- traveled and having a broad range of interests, I've developed a very special kind of spirituality.

This was my first Darkness Retreat and I learned about it from a friend who had gone through one. Immediately after hearing about it, I decided to do it. My wish and intention was to get away from all stimulus, relax, experience an inner journey, as well as find solutions for problems that were so far unsolvable.

My friend, who recommended the retreat, had a very difficult experience. His experience was incomparable to anything I had experienced before and I couldn't really imagine what would happen to me. I did have concerns, but not any fear. The most important for me was to gain more self-understanding and deal with any outcomes as they came, regardless of what they looked like. In my opinion, every personal experience is good because it's the experience itself that's important.

Beforehand, I read a study about the effects on humans who stay for long periods in darkness. It really didn't look so rosy. So I came up with strategies to maintain a certain amount of control over the situation. One of my ideas was to counter the lack of optical stimuli by increasing haptic stimuli through physical training and yoga exercises. Additionally I wanted to use meditation to strengthen my spirit, although I had no idea whether or not any of this would work.

During the Darkness Retreat, I went through 4 phases:

Days 1 - 3 (Phase 1): Relaxation to deep relaxation, phases of long, dreamless deep sleep, sleeping more than being awake. Sports, yoga and meditation during the waking state.

Days 3 - 5 (Phase 2): Intensive dreams that I contemplated during long periods of wakefulness. Intensive self-investigation, balancing the consciousness and unconscious. During the waking state, practicing sports, yoga and meditation.

Days 5 - 7 (Phase 3): Short naps, long wakefulness. For the most part, I stopped doing sports and yoga and instead switched between meditation and lucid dreaming. This was by far the best phase. I saw a kind of film being played out in front of my mind's eye where all of my problems and the corresponding solutions were listed. I didn't need to do anything or with any conscious effort, all the solutions flowed from my subconscious. It was completely coherent and to this very day, I'm working to implement them.

Days 8 - 10 (Phase 4): This was primarily a time of making sense of the things I experienced in the previous phases, as well as developing strategies. After Phase 3, I wanted to start implementing changes but Phase 4 was very important so that the effects wouldn't vanish like a storm in a teacup.

During the entire time I felt amazing. The 10 days in the Darkness Retreat was the best time of my life. Unlike my friend who referred me, I wasn't confronted with any difficult or shocking situations. Instead, I learned about the wonderful resources that were hidden within my innermost core.

The Darkness Retreat brought very extensive changes in my personal attitude toward the important areas of life. To this day, the effect has stayed with me. It basically changed my reality and I've already implemented many things. The moment I returned "to the light", I felt very sensitive, especially during the hours right after the Darkness Retreat. It felt like a kind of psychological pollution from the outside world. I would recommend a Darkness Retreat for those people who want inner peace and who want to tap into a new dimension of self-awareness in their life.

Stefan from Mazotos, Cyprus, Age 45

11-Day "Astral Travel and Spiritual Self-Awareness" Group Retreat in May 2013

I'm Stefan, 45 years young, living my life on the beautiful sunny island of Cyprus.

For over 25 years, I've been working with personal growth, spirituality and consciousness development and have completed various educational trainings and coaching sessions. I've received and developed an extensive knowledge of spiritual and universal laws that have enabled me to offer as much as I can as a healer and spiritual counsellor.

During my Darkness Retreat, I experienced profound transformation and the highest forms of healing power for soul work in my life. The Darkness Retreat provided me with the opportunity to deeply penetrate into my true being and connect with my soul.

This was my first retreat in the dark and I learned about it through Bharati. She felt that it was the right time and could be very good for me. I made my decision to do the retreat soon after my first Darkness Retreat informational meeting with her.

Regarding my wishes and intentions for the Darkness Retreat, I was incredibly open and curious about what was waiting for me in the dark and what would happen "there". Yet on the other hand, I had a deep desire for healing, transformation and clarity about my future path.

In preparation for the Darkness Retreat, I thought about everything that I would have to do: daily things like shaving, etc., how to work, create speech memos and how I was going to write in my journal in the dark when I couldn't see where I was writing. I didn't have any fears, doubts or insecurities. I had complete confidence and trust. Additionally, I watched Bharati's videos to receive more information. At the beginning of my Darkness Retreat I slept very extensively and caught up on my lack of sleep. The body and brain adjusted very slowly to the darkness. I even slept through lunch on the second or third day, which is very unusual for me.

At some point after reciting OM for a long time and listening to the OM box in my room for several days and nights, I suddenly realized and said, "I AM AN OM!" I felt perfectly connected and in resonance with this cosmic, sacred sound. Already on the second or third day, I started to see lights. I felt as if I was lying in a cave and the opening was above me. At first the lights were like single dots, then flashes of light and a dim light on the ceiling of what felt like a vaulted cave. On the eighth or ninth day, I saw my hand in the bathroom for a very short time. Then I had an opportunity to look at my entire life back to the age of 3. I was able to go through all the important stages in my life very consciously and have a closer look at them. During the Darkness Retreat there were times I felt very secure and trusting, yet at times I also felt alone. I think that during these moments it was my ego who was saying, slowly but surely, goodbye.

For me personally, the Darkness Retreat brought more clarity and consciousness. I received a confirmation that we are all souls on an earth journey with soul work to fulfill and this is the reason we have come into this life. The internal process that I experienced during the days in the Darkness Retreat was an incredibly deep dissolution that led me more and more to my true self. I became even closer to my fears and could completely transform and heal them after the stay in the Darkness Retreat.

The moment I returned "to the light" was a very unique and simply incredible experience that can happen only after the first time one experiences a Darkness Retreat. The colors in nature were incredibly intense. I jumped when I saw a daisy and it was such a blessing to feel the warm sunshine on my skin and face. I would recommend a Darkness Retreat to anyone who is on a spiritual path and wants to know their true self and being. It is a vacation from one's normal life to experience their higher self. A Darkness Retreat is the highest, most intense and fastest way for personal consciousness development. Actually for my next Darkness Retreat, I would like to do the 49-day process.

Uwe from Bonn, Germany, Age 56

21-Day Individual Retreat in September 2013

I am a certified social educationalist with additional qualifications. For 25 years I worked as a specialist in child and youth psychiatry and afterwards, had my own private practice. I give psychological counseling, coaching and hypnosis sessions and I am a founding member of the Association for Artworks KHB. In my spiritual life, I am a Diamond Way Buddhist.

My meditation and research on the internet paved the way for my first Darkness Retreat. As my interest grew, I knew it was something I wanted to experience. I decided to spend at least 21 days in complete darkness. I also wanted to do it with a healing fast of water and cassia fistula. I decided to limit external contact during the retreat to a minimum and figured that the best situation for me would be full isolation. Finally, I needed rest to explore my own mind, my own psyche. Yes, I did have expectations. I felt inspired to deepen certain meditation practices and also confront my fears. I wished to take this special time and approach it as a ritual - concluding parts of my life and starting fresh. I wanted to consciously tap into the core of my being and strengthen internal as well as external healing powers. These were my ideas before I went into the Darkness Retreat.

Already while planning and preparing for my retreat, I came across strong resistance. My decision was put to a very hard test and criticised by my professional circle of psychologists, as well as others who had normally stood by me in such matters. I had so many setbacks that at the end, I was simply on my own. This low point, which I had experienced before, was both enriching and strongly empowering.

I didn't do any specific preparations for the Darkness Retreat. I had a good assessment of my abilities from practicing Christian and Buddhist meditation and doing extreme periods of retreat. I already had some experience in isolation tanks, according to the method of John Lilli, and learned how a brain can react under strong sensory deprivation. Another part of my routine is annual fasting of up to 40 days. For me, going into darkness was a very natural next step on my life journey. After going through the challenges mentioned above, I went back into a very deep inner self-process and questioning to find out if doing this retreat was necessary and what my motivations were for doing it.

In the Darkness Retreat I experienced pure silence. For three days I had the feeling of sleeping very deeply with no dreaming. The darkness allowed me to get close to myself. After a while, hallucinations started happening and then I found myself in a silent room. Surprisingly, there were also phases of boredom which alternated with peacefulness and a sense of security. It was a feeling of abundance where I could get in touch with my inner light, in the darkness. My dreams were very lucid in the Darkness Retreat. I experienced strong life-like visions and also went through painful, physical purifications, always being able to return to the silence again. I used this time to make profound decisions.

By and large, the darkness felt quite pleasant through the long stretches. After all, I was in good company! During my Darkness Retreat, I could actually strengthen my meditative practice and become more internally centered. I simply embraced being and worked on the theme of my spiritual fulfillment. After a while I became familiar with Hindu teachings and felt their presence in my energy field. This was an enormous blessing for my work and ability to meet with others on the same level. In certain areas I felt an unexpected spiritual grounding that I've integrated into my everyday life. A feeling of gratitude and unconditional love flowed through every part of my body. I felt ever-present, simply in the "now".

When I went "back to the light" after the retreat, I felt like a drunken sailor strolling through a park in strong wind. My body coordination needed stabilizing. I was fascinated and enjoyed watching the grass swaying in the gentle breeze and wonderful little flowers that were so white, so graceful, so beautiful. I felt like sitting down and taking it all in, while simultaneously feeling that my brain was running at full speed and functioning at its optimal level. After three weeks in the darkness, it was a very intense experience. When I have time and money, I'll go back to do another Darkness Retreat.

Sieglinde from Cham, Switzerland, Age 60

10-Day Individual Retreat in November 2013

At this point in my life, I'm able to look back at 27 successful years working as a trainer and consciousness researcher. Parents, partners, children, friends, teachers were the agents in helping me find fulfillment in my life. They supported me and were always there in each moment given to me by the Universal Divine. Everyday I welcome new challenges. For me, life in all its forms is the teacher.

It was a few years ago that I learned from a friend about Darkness Retreats. After years of self-inquiry, I took the decision to do a darkness therapy as I felt it could be just the right help and support to gain more clarity and have a deeper understanding about the essence of life. I didn't have any particular wishes or intentions, I just let it flow. I had only joy, and no fears or worries. For me everything was very safe. To prepare for the Darkness Retreat, I was looking forward to have time to rest, get in contact with my true inner nature. I felt very open and curious for this self-discovery.

Within the first moments of going into the dark, a sphere of blue light started shining above my head. I felt very relaxed. Every day this light expanded in the room, like moonlight shining into the room. It stayed with me throughout the entire Darkness Retreat. On the fourth day, there was absolute darkness. The darkness was like a black bead moving downwards from the ceiling. I felt like I could no longer stand up straight and had to bend over to make my way to the toilet. In the end, I could only crawl on the ground. I was very frightened. On the fifth day, the scare was over. The room was filled with gentle moonlight and I felt calm once again.

I had dreams during the night. An infinite amount of many different dreams. There was one dream that was particularly impressive and lasting. It was a person hanging from a chandelier in a large reception hall. When I saw it, a voice said at the same time, "This is Sieglinde's giant ego". It must have been dying. That was an amazing day! I laid wide awake and motionless in my bed. At the same time, I could see many levels of myself, like passing through dense fog into different worlds. Sometimes during the day there were periods of boredom, but mainly I was busy with my dream analysis. There were always apparitions and flashes of light. Also worth mentioning, thc toilet in the bathroom appeared luminous and silvery.

Throughout the entire time in the retreat, my feelings were like a roller coaster. Everything was there. I also had a certain amount of time orientation due to the church bell ringing in the village and this felt very pleasant for me.

The Darkness Retreat gave me a deep understanding of myself, crystal clear visions and an experience of emptiness. Thoughts and feelings are part of my body, but not part of my true being. During the time in complete darkness, my external identity withdrew and I was simply there.

After the retreat, I went "back into the light". At that moment it was blinding and I was extremely sensitive to light. The colors were bright and strong and everything moved under my feet. Everything was alive. So as not to hurt my feet, I stepped from the meadow onto the pavement. That was a big moment. Very touching and moving.

The Darkness Retreat was the end of darkness, feeling half-asleep and suffering. For me, darkness therapy is a form of self-awareness, self-discovery and self-knowledge. People who are curious and interested in doing one should be stable and in good physical and mental condition, in order to process the experiences in the dark. There are also times of emptiness. Simply existing, without any narrative.

Elena from Germany

10-Day Darkness Retreat in July 2014

When I first heard of a Darkness Retreat, I was horrified that there was such a thing at all. Then I felt a deep compassion with the friend who had told me about it. I thought to myself, "How bad does it get in life that you would voluntarily do something like that?" I was horrified but also had a lot of respect and compassion for the people who wanted to go through a Darkness Retreat. I couldn't imagine why I would ever want to do one for myself someday. I must also admit that, quite frankly, I was simply afraid of the dark. I was in trouble if someone accidentally switched off the light and I found myself in a dark room.

After about 2 years, I heard about a Darkness Retreat and decided for myself to go into complete darkness for 10 days. I did this because I was looking for clarity and solutions to specific issues in my life. It was important for me to take the time to get close to these topics in silence. Far away from the over stimulus and a chance to focus inward, I saw an opportunity to get to the bottom of these themes and be at ease. I was searching for harmony and calmness.

It was clear that I experienced a lot of anxiety, very intensively, a few days before the Darkness Retreat. Later on during the retreat, I also became overwhelmed by the unknown and my insecurities I felt from these completely new experiences. When I think about my preparation for the retreat, I can tell you that from the day I registered, a certain inner process started happening. Several questions and concerns came up. Of course, I started to research more and read reports that also added to my fears about the unknown. I contacted my friend who had already gone through one. Speaking with him and also knowing that he had survived it, gave me an inner feeling of peace and calm.

During the Darkness Retreat itself, I experienced that all was simply bright from the appearance of inner light. I had an experience where I was told that I was safe and protected. Even today I still have this image in my mind. There were many insights, inner processes, emotions and more that one has to experience for themselves. In the dark I had the feeling of experiencing everything a person could feel. It was a space where everything was present.

Personally, the Darkness Retreat strengthened my spirit and being. Afterwards I was much more in touch with my feelings. Love and compassion for others as well as myself has grown. My awareness has expanded and I look at life very differently. My senses went through a healing and after the Darkness Retreat, they have all improved. My vision, sense of taste, touch, smell and hearing have all become better. This overall improvement has really added to the quality of my life.

The moment I came back to the light was simply overwhelming. It's hard to put into words. Upon my arrival at the Darkness Retreat, my counsellor told me how much people enjoy the beauty of the garden after the retreat. I must confess that at that time, although I found the garden nice, it wasn't like I was jumping up and down with euphoria. And then suddenly, after fifteen days in the Darkness Retreat, I came back to the light, saw the garden, and tears flowed as my eyes were grasping the overwhelming beauty of it all. I felt motionless for two or three hours and couldn't move from the awesomeness I saw in that moment. It was springtime and in addition, full moon. I went out into the garden shortly before sunrise. The clouds had the most beautiful motifs of animals, like horses. To give an example, I still have a strong memory of how fascinating it was to watch these images taking shape over and over. I couldn't believe what I saw. I felt as if I must have been completely blind before the Darkness Retreat. I don't even wear glasses and my ophthalmologist tested my vision as better than 100%! This moment made me very humble. I really felt like I needed to apologize that I never saw this before. But to whom or what could I give my apology? To myself, to life, the spirits, the universe, God or the angels? However it was to be, my tears were flowing. The brighter it became outside, the color of the grass and flowers started shining more and more around me. Everything appeared like bright neon-colored miracles of nature in a painting. Still overwhelmed and motionless, I just thought, "God, that is beautiful". I felt so alive in this fascinating world full of beauty. I just loved everything I saw and was impressed by the uniqueness and overwhelming beauty of it all. I could not have thought of changing anything at the place. Everything was already perfect, or imperfectly beautiful.

The Darkness Retreat experience has changed my life, especially through the healing of my senses. I'm able to give and receive much more love. The experience of the retreat awakened my humility before nature and life itself. This has made me feel more understanding, relaxed, patient and tolerant.

Dreschu from Berlin, Germany, Age 67

14-Day Individual Retreat in 2014

I am 67 years old, widowed and have two daughters. As a child, I grew up in East Berlin and went to school in West Berlin. I graduated from high school, studied aerospace technology and at the same time, I practiced yoga and meditation. Then the Wilhelm-Reich initiative, bodywork therapies, Bhagwan and self-help groups came into my life. After completing my studies I became a software developer. Even now that I'm already in my retirement years, I'm still working in IT. For me, the driving force in my lifetime has been to achieve balance between the competition of work, family life and spirituality, and to continue my spiritual growth even further.

This was my first and so far, my only Darkness Retreat. I found out about it on YouTube. The first time I actually heard about it was about 20 years ago. I read an article by Holger Kalweit in *Esotera* and I knew that it was something I wanted to experience. But over the years it didn't work out. It was only when I stumbled across a Darkness Retreat on Youtube that I finally took the decision. I had no wishes or intentions, I was just curious how I would deal with such a situation and what would happen to me. I found it tempting and exciting. I also did not have any fears or concerns. I was fulfilling a long cherished wish, yet I was uncertain of the unknown and about what to expect. I didn't really prepare for the Darkness Retreat except for practicing a few meditations.

For the first three days in the Darkness Retreat I slept for a long time. Then the dreams began. After waking up I could remember more and more details with up to five different dreams each night. Amongst them were interesting dreams showing me future events. For example, I dreamed of Edward Snowden and what would happen to him, or future events of the Darkness Retreat team. I learned later that a few times I also dreamed the same themes that a fellow Darkness Retreat participant, who was staying in the room next to me, had dreamed.

Once I had a vision where I was sitting and meditating above a snowy village, presumably in the Himalayas. The room had disappeared and I could see the landscape in all directions. It was an incredibly peaceful scene of absolute tranquility. In some of the small houses I could see light and everything was covered in snow. After a while, I closed this view of the valley with my eyes, like a fan being pushed back together, and came back in my room.

Once I saw in the room a very large female figure with blue skin color. Similar to the character in the movie Avatar, but Indian. It was very powerful how she appeared and grew before me, not threatening but very imposing. Then she disappeared. I had another impressive vision a week later when I could see through the wall of the entrance to the bathroom. The solid plaster appeared as a slatted fence with enough space between the slats that I could see through into the next room and it was all immersed in moonlight. But it was only visual, as I couldn't touch or feel the slats. Then I realized that this hallucination had twisted the true layout. The door of my room was actually next to this fake door and when I attempted to walk through it, I ended up running into the massive wall.

During the Darkness Retreat I felt deep relaxation and satisfaction. It was the perfect holiday. I didn't have to worry about food and could just spend my time thinking about different possibilities. I was finally out of my everyday stress and it felt amazing!

The Darkness Retreat gave me a full and complete rest and felt like having a curtain lightly lifted to see behind it and realize the potentials that were inside of me. First of all, I was always able to enjoy the peace and the "not having to do anything". I could fully let go and relax . I would have gladly stayed on for one week longer but unfortunately, it was fully booked for the next Darkness Retreat guests.

After two weeks of darkness and following the advice of Bharati, my Darkness Retreat counsellor, the first time I went out was on the evening before the last day. This helped me to slowly and carefully acclimate my eyes to seeing again. It was then surprising that all the white lights, such as the street lanterns, had an incredible powerful, stinging green color, like green traffic lights. When I looked at my arm, it seemed like it was constantly moving back and forth, although it felt calm resting on the chair. The airplanes were not flying as usual in a straight-line, but leapfrogging. Not only forward but also backward. I couldn't take any type of movement as being real, either with my arms and hands or with the airplanes. It was very strange.

It was also remarkable the next morning when I looked out the window. The inner glow from the plants totally blinded me. Everything, not only the blossoms but also the leaves, was shining and had extremely strong neon colors. I had to close my eyes again and again so as not to get overwhelmed by the incredible beauty. There was no pause of this intense glow. I had planned to drive back the next day but the feeling with my eyes open made me so dizzy that I needed an extra day to return to the light.

In retrospect, I can say that through this time in the Darkness Retreat, I have more inner peace. My outer life did not really change.

Personally, I think the Darkness Retreat could be recommended for anyone who is interested in the extra-ordinary and is not afraid of surprises. That being said, a Darkness Retreat participant should have inner stability. People who identify most importantly with the external and material are likely to have problems during the retreat when they are suddenly thrown into a situation with only themselves. It would be useful to have some knowledge about self-awareness and the inner life.

After this experience in the Darkness Retreat, I could imagine making a Darkness Retreat alone, without supervision. I believe I'll do it at some point in time but at the moment my focus is moving and settling down in Canada.

Sabine from Sasbachwalden, Germany, Age 58

6-Day Individual Retreat in September, 2016

My name is Sabine and I was born in Northern Germany. From the beginning of Bharati's Darkness Retreats, I have assisted and been part of the development. By assisting Bharati with the supervision and counseling, I was able to learn about some of the most exciting, intensive, profound and even life-changing experiences and transformations of the guests. It became clear that I wanted this as well for myself! I wanted to experience what I had only heard about and see what a Darkness Retreat would do for me. Additionally, and in order to take even better care of our guests, it was very important for me to understand how it feels go through a Darkness Retreat, especially afterwards.

I had absolutely no fears, concerns or insecurities and I didn't prepare at all. I was already familiar with all the organizational aspects, lived as a vegetarian for a long time, and just waited for whatever was to come. I took a voice recording device in order to be able to document situations or experiences. In hindsight, this was very helpful.

When I entered the darkness, I could switch off immediately. For two and a half days I only slept, with my eyes opening only for a moment to realize "oh it's still dark" and then back I went to sleeping. In between I had several interesting experiences which were more like astral travel experiences and less like a dream.

In one, I looked at the window on the wall and saw that a piece of black taping had come off and light was entering. "Damn", I thought I had already checked everything beforehand. I was too lazy to fix it immediately and thought, "Oh well, it's dark when I close my eyes and sleep so I'll just fix it later." To think about it, was to do it. So when I eventually woke up and felt my way up the wall to the window, it was a big surprise when I found it completely sealed and covered.

I had a very exciting telepathic experience in which I heard Bharati saying something in a meeting and coming to an agreement with someone. This couldn't have been possible as she was at the other end of the house. However, later on during our conversation she confirmed that she had actually had this discussion.

Also several light experiences were very exciting. Sometimes everything became bright right in front of me, like a mist. I could tell if this had been light that came in through a window, but there was no light entering from anywhere. Whenever I wanted this misty light to remain in the room, it disappeared. Once in the bathroom a very bright spotlight shined for several minutes.

Several times I dreamed that I was running through the house in the light and thought to myself: "Oh I need to hurry and get back in the room, no one can know that I'm walking around out here" or another dream with a lot of people partying in my room and I had to say, "Hey guys, could you please disappear now?" I also tried to put on my sleeping mask but unfortunately, it was transparent. That was very funny! In another experience, I complained to a colleague because she hadn't properly taped the windows.

The most impressive experience was my visit to the akashic records where I received information about past lives and my relationship with people in this life. To find out more information about the city of Worms, I searched the internet and then found the actual documents which confirmed my astral experience.

The daily conversations with Bharati gave me many insights about how I could deal with some of the processes. Among other things, insight about the internal transformation taking place as each layer peeled off like an onion and revealed the next thing that needed to be solved. The most important thing, among many treasures, was definitely how much I came to value silence. No speaking, no phone calls, no responses needed. However, my intention to have a day of silence once a week has unfortunately gotten stuck.

The moment I returned to the light was very intense and impressionable. It was in the morning and the sun was shining. The colors of the flowers were extremely colorful and I couldn't get enough of it. Afterwards, I felt a bit dizzy and wanted to lie down. It would have been great if I had more time to ease back into my daily life but I had to get back to my work right away as the sole counsellor and supervisor for an American guest.

After the retreat I had a much better understanding of the reactions experienced by the guests. There wasn't one moment where I had to think about whether or not I would do the Darkness Retreat counsellor training. Already at this time it was quite clear that this would be part of my life path. I warmly recommend Darkness Retreats to everyone who is searching to reach their inner essence, who has a yearning for spiritual growth or just wants to get away from all external Influences and communicate with themselves.

Benergy from Aachen, Germany, Age 38

10-Day Individual Retreat in January 2015

Hello, I'm Benergy! I completed the Darkness Retreat at the beginning of a six-month sabbatical. I guess my first thought was that I should, "Eat that frog!" I had quite a bit of respect and appreciation for the darkness and wanted to put this at the very beginning of my professional break. After all, it would be my first retreat in complete darkness. I simply wanted the experience and see what it would do for me. Right at the very beginning of my time off, I had the idea to let go of the old and open up to new experiences within a relatively short period time. I also had some things that I wanted to heal.

Prior to the retreat, I was a bit afraid of the dark. It reminded me of the time when I felt insecure as a child, going into a dark cellar to get a jar of plums. I was already familiar with my retreat room as I had stayed there on New Year's Eve. That was really the only preparation I had.

As I finally went into the Darkness Retreat, I had a very intense feeling in my body that was not particularly pleasant. However through yoga and meditation, it became better. The darkness, as it felt there, was no problem at all and I didn't have any fears about it. Before,

I wondered how great the temptation would be to cheat. There was a window that I opened everyday for fresh air so naturally, light entered into the room. I wore an eye mask which prevented seeing any outside light. I was very relieved that I had absolutely no desire to cheat and wanted to stay in the dark. My meditations went very deep, penetrating and accessing faraway worlds - very freaky! More and more my inner light emerged, which I could see in myself.

In the Darkness Retreat, a process picks you up wherever you are on your path. It's not always pleasant. Originally I wanted to stay only seven days but then extended to ten days. It took me a while to get used to the new, dark environment. Additionally, I stayed in a shared flat which means I heard the other guests. Theoretically you could also speak in the hallways, but I didn't want to. All the doors, except for the bathroom, were not lockable. At first I found it a bit strange, even if no one sees anything.

The Darkness Retreat gave me a lot. The darkness became my friend. She gave me self-confidence because I had to overcome my fear and experience some important things. I feel that the Darkness Retreat is a type of spiritual incubator. It is an inner journey into the unknown. At the end however, you always end up with yourself. The mantras helped me to build up spiritual energy and from time to time, I dove into past incarnations. The soul took the opportunity to thoroughly clean up.

The moment I returned back into the light was magical. I was surrounded by light beings who accompanied me out of the darkness. However, I myself didn't notice them at first. Bharati had taken photos for my blog and they appeared very clearly. It was beautiful to be able to decide myself at which moment I wanted to come back into the light. The colors were super intense and I found the world so incredibly beautiful. The themes from past incarnations stayed with me for quite some time after the Darkness Retreat. In the end, I travelled for several months and many people were interested in how it was in the darkness.

I would recommend a Darkness Retreat to anyone who is looking for something without knowing exactly what it is. All the answers are within us. The art is to perceive, accept and implement them. Be your own guru!

Hermann from Lübbecke, Germany

11-Day Individual Retreat in January 2015

During the Darkness Retreat I saw a lot of light flashes. It was interesting that even after many days in the retreat, I had a hard time finding my way around the 25 square meter room and at times found it extremely difficult to find my bed. It was an adventure just getting to the toilet because I often saw walls that didn't even exist. I had to use my hands to feel the walls that actually were there.

Once I had a very strange experience. While I was very dazed, the room suddenly lit up. I was quite confused and thought something had happened because otherwise everything was pitch dark. Above me, I clearly saw an intricately carved beam ceiling but in the blink of an eye, everything dipped into deep darkness once again. I've never experienced such a thing, before or after. The flashes of light, which I saw fairly regularly, were like permanent light beams. It was as if flashlights were attached to my head showing me objects that actually did not exist. Occasionally a reddish light appeared from my hands and forehead, like in the early photo labs. This light illuminated walls that were not there. I discussed this phenomenon several times with Bharati and she suspected that the strong, magical charge of her house could have led to this strange phenomena.

During this time I hoped that I would learn something more about my past lives but unfortunately, this wish wasn't fulfilled as much as I dreamed it would be.

Nikolaus from Aachen, Germany

17-Day Individual Retreat in March 2015

It is very hard for me to write down my thoughts. Especially on the computer because it makes me very tired. But I want to let you know one thing, it was a very special experience for me to spend 17 days fasting (water and tea) in the dark, and to have felt well for most of the time. However during the last few days, I also drank vegetable broths due to having headaches from salt withdrawal.

At the beginning of the retreat, I feared that I would be harshly confronted with inner fears. But in fact, it turned out to be a time of deep relaxation and curiosity. In the dark I learned and experienced the differences between astral travels and dreams. This was a very valuable experience for me. I never regretted, not even for one minute, to have done the Darkness Retreat. If I want to do it again, I could imagine staying longer in the dark.

Petra from Deiningen, Germany, Age 54

7-Day "Astral Travel and Spiritual Self-Awareness" Group Retreat in May 2015

It was through the internet that I learned about this possibility. I went to Bad Dürrheim for a darkness meditation and then decided to do a Darkness Retreat. I was very curious about it and wished for changes that would make my life better. But I also felt that my expectations and wishes were once again, set too high.

I didn't have any fear and during the first days, I didn't experience anything as my curiosity centered on who was in the group. On the fourth day I was a bit afraid as the walls appeared to close in and move around my bed. On the fifth day it was the same. I also saw two figures on the wall but I couldn't tell what or who it was. In the outer hallway I saw the white walls leading to the common room and in the toilet were flashes of light appearing on the wall.

In the beginning it was very relaxing for me, since before I had a lot of stress. Then unfortunately I no longer had so many experiences and it became a bit boring. I wanted some entertainment. On the sixth day I had a panic attack and lost my breath. I longed for fresh air, things worsened and I couldn't breathe properly. For this reason I stopped my Darkness Retreat on the day before the last day, but then had a feeling that it was the wrong decision.

The moment I returned "to the light" again, it felt very nice to see again. The colors were brighter and stronger. During the first few days back home I felt an inner satisfaction. But that changed as I quickly got caught up in everyday life again. In my opinion, nothing changed in my life. Nevertheless, it was a new experience for me to make everything in the dark and find my way.

It's difficult for me to give a recommendation for a Darkness Retreat. Everyone should decide for themselves whether they want to experience a Darkness Retreat. We humans are all different - some like it, others are not yet ready for it.

Odette from Bern, Switzerland, Age 52

10-Day Individual Retreat in May 2015

My name is Odette. I live in Bern, Switzerland. My present professional activities are cooking and taking care of a holiday island. During the school holidays I dedicate myself to a children's program. I'm very interested in herbs, medicinal plants and for many years I've been producing a wild garlic paste that I sell to organic food stores in and around Bern. Since many years I practice shiatsu and yoga. I enjoy travelling, especially to Asia, and am always learning something new. I am particularly interested in yoga, ayurveda and much more.

This was my first Darkness Retreat.

Since years, I've practiced teachings from Bön Buddhism. In this tradition, a Darkness Retreat is also recommended with practical texts from ancient and modern times. As I was searching YouTube for newer reports, I discovered Bharati. The video convinced me right away and I signed up immediately. Actually, I had no major wishes and just wanted to see what would happen. But I also had fears.

By and large, I didn't make any significant preparations except that I packed my temple, a bamboo flute, painting tools and a yoga mat. During the first three to four days in the Darkness Retreat, I let the OM box run so I would be more calm and eliminate any anxiety. As far as I remember, I was very tired during that time and I slept a lot.

On the fourth or fifth day I saw very subtle, bright blue lights. I sang many mantras. During this time I was dealing with being caught up in problematic love story with a man from Sri Lanka. This man ran away, lied and deceived me in financial matters. I felt imprisoned by the whole story and talked about it with Bharati. In doing so, I realized that there are people who use certain practices to manipulate other people. I had to solve it on a deep internal level. So I worked on letting go, and letting go. This was a first and profound step. I really treasured the daily conversations with Bharati.

After the Darkness Retreat, I attended a seminar with my Buddhist teacher in Switzerland. Then I had a very strong dream. From my left side, an enormous, squealing monster came out of my body. I understood that there was something in me that had to do with this man from Sri Lanka. But now, let's get back to the Darkness Retreat. Around the sixth day, I saw Yantras, the sacred geometric diagrams. The patterns were everywhere and colorful. These were amazing moments. There were also days when I wanted to get out and had no desire to continue and stay until the end. I always looked forward to the counseling discussions and since you don't see or feel the other person, the connection at the soul level is very strong.

When I did go out, the daylight was very extreme. I needed two to three hours just to get used to it. I also felt very weak and had to drink a broth right away. From then, it was upwards and onwards. The entire experience in the Darkness Retreat was interesting, but I was happy to return to the light again. The moment I returned to the light, everything dazzled. The natural colors were very intense. Yes it felt very good to be back in the light but in hindsight, I realized that it was only through the darkness that I became deeply close to myself.

I can recommend a Darkness Retreat experience to anyone who would like to go deep within themselves.

Susanne from Mühledorf, Switzerland, Age 63

8-Day Silent and Stillness Group Retreat in May 2015

Meditation has been a part of my life for 50 years and belongs to my everyday routine like eating, drinking and sleeping. I wanted to do a Darkness Retreat since a long time but thought I would have to travel to Asia. When I heard about Bharati and her offerings in Germany, I knew immediately that I wanted to go there. I knew from my experience of doing around 60 silent retreats that sensory channels become strengthened and I imagined this would be even more the case since the eyes do not need to, nor can they, see anything. I also wanted to discover interdimensional travel. I had no fears, concerns or insecurities.

I felt very awful in the dark. I didn't expect this at all. The shape of the rooms were different and much larger than expected. I landed twice in the wrong room because I just couldn't find my way. My senses were flipping and I was doing spiritual somersaults, depending on what I was thinking or what mantra I was trying. The spiritual forces became stronger and I could communicate easily with beings from other dimensions, but had trouble participating actively in discussions at the table during the group gatherings. My thoughts were constantly wandering off.

I remember being nervous in the beginning. I had trouble staying grounded. Then I received direct help from a spirit friend who suddenly appeared and asked if he could help me. From that moment my energies were balanced and I could enjoy the retreat. I was not bored either and in the end I found the time too short. I appreciated the fact that I was able to go through my own process. I was very sensitive to noise and muted everything that I could. Knowing that the bell would ring at some time and signal for our group to meet, was the only sound I tolerated.

The Darkness Retreat showed me once again that I have everything within myself and only need to open up to understand infinite, new worlds. After the retreat I went home, a little drunk on the amazing colors I saw afterwards, and immediately started working again. I now realize that I could go through a longer period of darkness without problems and feel wonderful, whether alone or in a group. As mentioned above, I had a nervous phase during which I could hardly find any peace. That was challenging. The help came miraculously from another dimension. I was able to release myself to the process, allowing whatever needed to happen and whatever it wanted to show me. For me, both Darkness Retreats and Silent Retreats are similar and I feel incredibly grateful to have been given these opportunities to explore the deepest and most hidden corners of my being. The moment I returned to the light was very intense. I was warned to be careful and slowly get used to the light so I could enjoy the intense colors in nature for as long as possible. Never had I seen nature so beautiful! An image that will always remain in my mind is when I saw a wonderful, soft, violet cornfield, planted next to a sports field, with ears of corn growing 40 - 50 cm high. The flowery meadows which I passed on my way to Switzerland, with golden birds that flew amongst intensely and multicolored trees can't be described in this limited space.

The retreat changed my life through the expansion and perception of interdimensionality which I've integrated this into my everyday life and use it consciously. It's hard to say to whom I would recommend a Darkness Retreat. There should be an inner desire, a longing for something greater in yourself which can reveal itself most of all when it becomes silent, and dark. Why do it? Because it can be a blessing for spiritual growth and moving forward on our path. At the moment I'm not planning to do another Darkness Retreat, I'm still feeling fulfilled from the last time!

Birgit from Zurich, Switzerland

11-Day Individual Silent Retreat in January 2016

My name is Birgit. I am a healer and I support and counsel people on their life path. I use different techniques for energetic healing combined with psychology and personal development. I feel it's my responsibility to support people in their process, to help them find the connection to themselves and take responsibility to follow their own path.

One day I read about the ancient tradition of retreating in a dark cave for a long period of time and thought there must be something like that today. So I went on a search. For years I was always thinking about the idea and for a long time I couldn't find anything suitable for me. Then I came across Spiritbalance and I clearly knew that I had found the right place.

Before heading into the retreat, I came up with ideas and wishes for what I wanted during this time in complete darkness. I spent time checking if I still had buried patterns and fears in my life that I didn't face in my daily life. I didn't have any doubts or worries about my decision. Three days before I began preparations for my retreat by switching to light food so I could feel clean and clear. In the Darkness Retreat I started my process very quickly, within hours. I experienced a great calm within myself and looked at the different stages of my life. I hardly slept in the beginning, since I had been eating very lightly for five days and when I did sleep, it was a short phase of very intense dreaming (like a short afternoon nap). It helped me to look at the various topics.

From the beginning I saw a lot of light flashes and light beings. After a while, I had a precise idea about the space I was in which had nothing to do with the physical reality. I found this very fascinating. And I could tell by the energy field whether it was day or night. This was another nice experience. In the dark I felt very comfortable, secure, connected and totally relaxed.

It was overwhelming to go from the Darkness Retreat back into the light again. There was a lot of snow so the light was glistening brightly. For me personally, the Darkness Retreat brought more clarity. I found out for myself where I stand. It confirmed my path. I would also recommend a Darkness Retreat to everyone. I think it is helpful for all of us to spend time with ourselves and consciously deal with our thoughts.

Hans-Joachim from Speyer, Germany

11-Day Individual Retreat in March 2016

I planned my retreat so that I would arrive on Saturday, the 19th of March, have one day to familiarize myself with my room and surroundings in the light and then on Sunday the 20th, begin my Darkness Retreat.

The first time I came across the topic of a Darkness Retreat was at least 15 years ago from Holger Kalweit. I found the experiences of the participants so interesting that I decided, "I'm going to do that too!" Among other things, it was pointed out in many of the personal experience reports that the participants experienced being in touch with their inner light. At this time I had already embarked on spiritual journey and read the brochure which I still have today, completely faded and barely legible. My beginner's enthusiasm failed due to lack of time and money, which everyone is familiar with. However what did happen, was that every three to four years the subject of a Darkness Retreat appeared in my life in one way or another. 2016 was finally my time and so now, here I am writing down my experiences.

Beforehand, I spoke with Martin and he suggested that it would be an advantage to start the retreat on the same day of my arrival, which I then did.

On the first day I entered into the dark very consciously. It was a strange sensation when I opened my eyes and in spite of knowing better, my internal reflex expected to see something or a visual image. This didn't happen, it was absolute darkness. The sensations were characterized by calm, silence and security. All that was outside of this room didn't matter to me at all. I felt that even if a bomb had gone off, it wouldn't have affected me.

Before I continue with my report, there is something that I must mention. I asked Bharati, my spiritual counsellor during the Darkness Retreat, to take an aura and chakra photograph before and after my stay in complete darkness. I was very surprised, yet somehow not, that the most open chakra was my crown chakra. All other chakras were open to different degrees.

On Sunday, the first day, not much more really happened. I had brought three technical devices with me. A voice recorder to record my impressions so I wouldn't forget them, a portable CD player to listen to gentle meditative sounds and a walkman with different music tapes.

So, what happened? My CD player gave up after the second CD and my walkman was jammed and I couldn't take out the tape. The only thing that worked was my voice recorder. Later I learned from Bharati that electrical equipment frequently stops functioning during a retreat. I just saw this as a sign that I shouldn't distract myself. All this had been settled for me.

That night as I was half-asleep, I didn't know exactly whether I was actually thinking or dreaming but I was inspired to write a book. I also saw the title of the book before my very eyes. It was versed in a theme such as: "How Life Works" or "The One who Went Out to Find Himself". Whatever happened after that, disappeared. Suddenly, a film played in my mind about my entire life beginning from the age of two until my forties and fifties. The details and particularities were true, with people, specific events and experiences that I had long forgotten. Everything was there and so real to me as if I had just experienced it. This incident was so impressionable that I woke up and thought about what had just happened. The next morning I felt very well rested. I decided to meditate and wanted to go into this silence and see my inner light. This was one of my main reasons to do the Darkness Retreat.

I noticed how I would easily let myself become distracted from the outside and how nice it was to hear the village church bell ring. But at the same time I also knew that these distractions were disturbing my self-discovery process. So I told myself that it was important to go into silence and not get distracted. But I also just calmed down and said to myself: "Ok it's only the second day, let's just wait and see what happens." I felt a strong need to get in touch with my soul and expressed this desire out loud. As soon as I said it, I received a rather amusing and ironic answer in the form of thoughts: "I really don't know what you want. We're in touch with each other all the time. When you become aware of me, the invisible guide, you're connected. Then you and I are one. Whenever you are consciously thinking of me, I'm there for you. You are the one who thinks, feels and acts as you wish. I'm always with you, watching how you evolve and how you become the highest expression of yourself." I must tell you, it was a very weird feeling. I had asked a question and then gave myself the answer. Naturally I wanted to know why it felt awkward and strange that the answer had come from myself. Right after this thought, came the answer: "As long as you still have so many patterns of belief and ideas of separation in your energy system, this will continue to be so. But don't worry about it, you are on a very good path."

One of the next days was full moon. During this day, all of Bharati's Darkness Retreat participants along with six other people from her meditation circle were invited to participate in a Light Meditation. In the dark, of course. She explained to us that during the time of new and full moons, energy portals open up to other worlds, both higher and lower, and the energy flows more strongly into our universe than it does at other times. Afterwards, we chanted together the Graceful Light or Rainbow Mantra (Arut Perum Jothi Arut Perum Jothi Thani Perum Karunai

Arut Perum Jothi) to send light into the world. Another mantra (Om Namah Shivaya) helped us bring the five elements (earth, fire, sky, water, air) into harmony within ourselves and with everything. That night I had two very intense dreams, which I prefer not to discuss because they are very personal and connected to my life.

The fifth day was my total personal crisis day. Perhaps the word "crisis" is somewhat exaggerated. Actually, my day of irritation and resistance is better. So what happened?

On this day everything and everyone annoyed and disturbed me. It started when I had opened the window to get some fresh air and heard the church bell ring, the twittering birds, the stories being told by people on the street and especially Nam Hari, who was chanting mantras (as usual) in the room next door. I wanted to shake him. This was very unusual because I really enjoyed his mantra chanting during the days before and after. It resonated in me and always felt very soothing. Here it was the exact opposite.

When I got up the next morning and wanted to put on my socks, I felt a strong need to do something good for my feet. So I gave them a massage and had a wonderful conversation with them about paying attention and being mindful. It was really astonishing how much I took certain things for granted, although that's probably just particular for me as I'm sure others are more aware of their body than I am. It was just very new for me to realize, in a whole new and obvious way, how much I had strained my feet. After all, I've been extremely overweight for a very long time in my life.

This was also the second day where I had a long, enlightening conversation with Bharati. She told me about her astral travels and I told her about my aspirations and inspirations. Through the conversation, we discovered that the circumstances in my life were similar to one of her friends and she absolutely wanted to bring us together. She felt that it could be a great support.

The last night I had a very intense dream about my deceased mother and me. It was, as you say in slang, "hardcore". I felt joyful as I thought about all that awaited me in the future and about being able to go back into the light the next morning.

In the temple room, I lifted my eye mask little by little to slowly bring more light onto my eyelids until finally I could completely remove my eye mask and open my eyes completely. Wow, the thought of how strenuous it felt - even exhausting - shot through my head. I wasn't at all aware of how much energy is consumed from seeing. Although when I thought about it, I realized how many visual impressions the brain has to constantly deal with. I immediately closed my eyes again to keep the energy, which was very pleasant and relaxing. Then I went to the mirror and looked into my eyes. What I saw brought tears rolling over my cheeks. From my eyes radiated so much warmth and love that I cried with joy. I felt a little dizzy while standing and went back to sit in my chair. This feeling lasted for about half an hour until everything normalized again.

In closing, I would like to say that I can recommend a Darkness Retreat to anyone who is a seeker, or as Neale Donald Walsch puts it, a "remembering member." And of course, only for those who are attracted and feel a resonance to do it. In my life I often make up new mottos, one of which is, "It is how it is, and when it changes, that's again how it is!" This retreat gave me a new motto: "Everything can be, but nothing must be!" For me, this understanding had a new and profound meaning.

I wish all those who are on their journey to never stop in front of any obstacle. To those who have not yet set out, I wish for their life struggles to shake them so much that they have to take a break and become aware that a "journey" would do them good.

Matthias from Kaiserslautern, Germany

10-Day Individual Retreat in May 2016

I experienced a Darkness Retreat for the first time at an Open Door event in Oberbaldingen and decided shortly afterwards that I would go into the dark. My wishes were, on one hand, to learn about astral travel, and on the other hand, I was afraid of the dark and wanted to get over that. In spite of my fears, I didn't really do any preparation for the Darkness Retreat.

My experience in the Darkness Retreat was filled every day with strong visions, dreams, as well as astral travel. I felt relaxed and could think a lot about myself, gradually gaining a new perspective of my life. I was able to process many fears and learned to let go of them. The moment I "went to the light" again was painful. Since the Darkness Retreat, I've become more conscious of myself. For example, I don't lie or deny that I eat chocolate, I just go ahead and eat it. In general, I would recommend a Darkness Retreat to anyone who is on a path to find their true inner self.

Peter from Göttingen, Germany

10-Day Individual Retreat in June - July, 2016

To this day, the Darkness Retreat has had a very strong influence on me. It was especially at the end of my retreat and immediately following that I realized how much fear I was living with in the world. I became more closely connected to my fears and was able to see that the strategies I normally used to combat those fears were no longer working so well. For me this process was very beneficial. Now I'm more in touch with my feelings, less afraid to face my fears and as well as other feelings.

This may sound as if I'm full of fear and can't even stand on my feet. It's actually just the opposite. I'm a very successful psychotherapist, seminar leader, trainer and company consultant. What I really want to convey is that I've finally managed to actually work through the fear in myself and am able to feel it without becoming overwhelmed.

Emotions are an ancient language, first came smell, touch, gesture and more. The emotional world for us mammals is a very important language, which is hardly valued in our culture today. And seemingly opposite of this, we're very afraid to express our feelings. Often it's not a matter of what it's connected to, it's the intensity of the feeling. Be it joy, shame, fear or anger.

My purpose for the Darkness Retreat was to get in touch with the very, very small inner child and slowly, but surely, resolve any trauma. Traumas are the result of being in a difficult life situation where we are no longer able to let the energy of emotions flow through us. As a child we need, at the very least, a very trusting person such as our mother, who can comfort us and accepts that we are afraid even though they themselves can't take the pain away or make it disappear. The Darkness Retreat was very beneficial and I will do it again. When exactly, I don't know yet. There are also a few of my clients who would like to experience going into the dark for a few days.

Overall, it was a very impressive experience. I wasn't overwhelmed but there were always new things that appeared within the daily 20-hour process. After a few days, I saw things that were not there at all before. Then a few days later in the evening, I sat down on the couch and had visions. There were new images constantly passing in front of my inner eye. It didn't matter whether my eyes were open or closed, the images simply passed by. Bharati told me that they were astral images which appear after a few days to some of the participants. Often I was in the sea and it was light. Even though no light entered my eyes during those nine days, it felt like daytime. I saw three-dimensional trees and shrubs that were extremely alive growing right before my eyes. These images were constantly moving and passing in front of me, even when I was sitting and eating at the table. And then my internal resistance would show up telling me that these were just more new tricks being played in my mind to distract me from going deeper into my uncomfortable feelings. By the way, we were eating only raw food and I ate less and less, eventually having no hunger. In the beginning I wasn't able to connect to myself at all. I felt like I was functioning only according to the normal structures of eating, lying down and meditating. Things went very slowly because I felt lost and disoriented in my room. This feeling was a big help to do a lot of work with my inner child.

The visions or hallucinations occurred nearly all the time. For example, I saw a lot of bicycles in my room, one above the other, or hanging from the ceiling. All of them had a spiral cable attached to the luggage rack, which was mounted very high. There were also children's bikes. And then after it was over, I had a light and calm feeling. Another time, wooden beams, like those used in half-timbered houses appeared very suddenly out of nowhere. Again and again I had to duck and dodge the beams, even though they were not there at all. To find my through them, I really had to concentrate on where I wanted to go. The same thing happened with laundry that hung in the room. I could barely pass through it. Many of these moving rooms were filled with water. In one of them, a gigantic fish swam up to my nose and looked directly into my eye. If you always believe what you see, it can be very scary.

I often saw light flickering in my eyes and sometimes I felt a bit dizzy but I must say, I was never afraid of it. I found it really funny that even though I knew these things existed only in my mind and weren't real, I was still constantly ducking my head as I walked through the room. On top of the dresser that I used for my clothes, I saw a lot of glasses. They were tall, crystal glasses that took up the entire space and I didn't know where to put my things. But sometimes when I set my things down, the images would change. During the first days I often saw old, decaying buildings, old factories, washed-out natural stone walls and much more.

At the end it was really a lot for me. All of the experiences, returning back into the light and then back again into the dark, where at first the illusions were still there and then disappeared. By the way, I always saw a red background color. Everything seemed to be soaked in red. Bharati said that this might have to do with a very open root chakra. I also thought I could see a window, but when I turned in another direction it was just as bright. Sometimes I saw my hands in front of my eyes. Wrong again. I only thought that I saw them. My mind was just creating an image for my hands to pass through. That's how I felt with most of these images. As soon as I had an idea of what something would look like, I could build a vision of it. It wasn't intentional but it was also not forced.

Sometimes light appeared in my eye from the side, both left and right. At times, I saw these apparitions in front of only one of my eyes and what I saw with my other eye also seemed correct. Then it would change eyes and other images would appear. And sometimes I saw everything before both eyes. It was interesting to feel how it was easy to simultaneously see images in one eye and nothing in the other. Sometimes I saw the shadow of my body on the wall, it felt as if the light came from behind me. Some nights I woke up at what felt like 2 am and I would work for two to three hours, for example practicing kundalini shaking meditations. After that I lied back down and around two hours later started again.

I can tell you that I never imagined how deeply I would look at the traumatics events in my life, which is exactly what I wanted. I think many people resolve their traumas just by feeling and then self-interpreting that the trauma has been resolved, yet in order for trauma to heal itself, one needs to get in contact with it. When one can go through the deep sorrow, cry and internally say yes to truly accept the process, the trauma is resolved. Although at the same time, the imprint of the mental trauma in the body does not necessarily become resolved. From that point, it means that it's no longer a matter of resolving the trauma, rather it requires recognizing that the physical symptoms are no longer correct and reprogramming is needed. The brain needs around 41 days to take hold of new patterns or rewrite the old pattern.

I went through most of the process by myself and some of it with Bharati, who was there as my counsellor for the 6 days. The worst thing for me was the lack of physical contact with other people. Getting used to this feeling of being alone was challenging and I was rather surprised how aware I became that I was avoiding it. Now, after just a few days back in the world, I already feel much less by myself.

On the last nights after dinner, I would always cry. Not right away in the beginning, but when I did it with intention and a bit of pressure, I would start crying. A deep sorrow that touched all sorts of things. For example, thinking about my grandmother's dog when I left the children's home and went to live with her touched me very deeply. As a 2-year-old child, I would lay in the dog's bed with the other puppies. Now I realized that I never cried over her death. Many personal hardships came up which I had never mourned before. Also the sadness of my grandfather's death was a process for me. When my grandfather died, I was 16 years old and away on a church holiday in Norway. At this time I couldn't cry because I just didn't feel anything. Now it had become so present that I was crying gallons of tears and at the same time, it felt very good to do so.

As an infant, I was always given a full baby bottle to keep me silent until I finally fell asleep. This means, that for a very long time I never felt anything while I was eating. It was a simple conditioning. Now I've become aware of this and actively go against this conditioning. The realization often came to me right after the meal. I ate, now I could cry a little! So I did and felt increasingly lighter. There were enough good reasons for me to cry. I cried about the soldiers from the second world war who had to fight but didn't want to. This came up because I remembered my older sister singing "I am always sad to bid you farewell, my brothers in arms..." and I was always sad when she sang this at night in our shared bedroom. I was also very touched when I listened to the song, "Where Have All the Flowers Gone".

After crying over the soldiers, I thought it was over and that I didn't have to cry anymore. But there were other things in the world, such as the Jewish Holocaust. Once while crying I saw an elderly couple in the gas chamber who had given up and simply sat down against one wall and died. I cried very much at this image.

In the Darkness Retreat, I learned to cry again. I can also handle being alone with myself, which I couldn't do so well before. At the end I often had very cold feet, as if my sole was made out of a thin layer of ice, and I had a similar sensation in my throat. Hour after hour I would try to warm up from the inside by attempting to light my internal fire.

Once when I was very angry at the way Bharati had spoken to me, I layed down on the bed feeling the deepest depths of this anger and really struggled with everything. Afterwards I felt a wonderful warmth, first in my feet and gradually rising upwards through my entire body. I stayed there in my bed lying motionless on my back for at least 1 to 1.5 hours.

I was never bored. However, from time to time it became increasingly difficult to stay in this cave. I had all sorts of ideas about how good it was on the outside. When I heard motorcycles passing by, which happened again and again in good weather, I thought of buying a scooter. My mind always wanted to divert my attention, yet most of the time I saw it right away. So I would focus on my inner mission: to connect the parts of me that I couldn't feel with those that I could. I was very disciplined about this.

I could continue to write for hours about my experience because there is just so much that I went through, but the memories have already faded away in some places. In absolute darkness, life is like a dream.

Matthias from Zurich, Switzerland

3-Day Individual Retreat in July 2016

This was a fantastic journey. Just the thought of three days in absolute darkness, with all of my insecurities and not knowing what would happen to me, gave me a strange feeling. I imagined everything possible but the actual experience was beyond any imagination. No doubt, it was one of the most beautiful experiences I've ever had.

Upon my arrival at the retreat center, I met very extraordinary people whom I had never met before. Nevertheless, it felt very familiar. Dear and lovely Sabine was there to welcome me. Her presence felt very motherly, open-minded and without prejudice. She was simply perfect and 100% present. It was so pleasant that I could really relax. In general, I felt very comfortable on the day of arrival. In the days before, I felt a lot of strong uncertainty but it was just wiped out on this day.

After a brief welcome, she showed me my room. As I arrived in the darkened room I noticed what a nice impression the room made on me. The creaking floor, the nice bed, the sofa, the chest of drawers, the shower and a washbasin was all at hand, as if it were a guesthouse for a country gentleman. But now it was a room to experience absolute darkness. The windows were covered with black foil and black tape so that no light could penetrate. The light switch was also fixed so I couldn't accidentally push it and switch on the light. Settling in the room and getting a quick feeling of trust in the space was necessary to find my way in the dark. I went through the room again and again so I could remember the location of the shower and the sink.

After a brief moment of silence with myself, I met Bharati. Together we prepared to let go of the light and slip into the darkness. All windows were now closed and the light completely turned off. The only physical light was Bharati's lotus flower, in which a candle burned. We talked for about an hour discussing various things and at the conclusion of our conversation, and as a beginning for the Darkness Retreat, Bharati sang a short, bright song for me about merging with the light. It was wonderful and at the same time I was so nervous.

Bharati left the room and it was time. I just sat there. It's funny when you sit in a dark room on a Friday afternoon at 4:00 pm and do nothing. I remember exactly how I was sitting there thinking, "what do I do now?" No mobile phone, no light, no book, nothing. I only had myself and my own thoughts and feelings. After a few minutes I became extremely tired and went to bed. After a while later I woke up from sleeping and didn't know how long I had slept. Was it 10 minutes or 6 hours? I simply had no idea because I didn't have a watch or phone. So I just went back to sleep. That first night I had deep dreams that worked on themes that had unconsciously burdened me for a long time. A big theme for me was the subject of fear. Specifically, fear of loss. This became apparent in my dreams during the first night.

Later on I woke up again and just sat there, thinking and thinking. My head was very noisy. For the first time I really saw what was going on inside me. My awareness was simply more inward because there was no stimulus from the outside.

After sitting for a long time, I took a shower, went to the toilet and brushed my teeth. I remembered that I had arranged with Sabine to bring me a cup of tea again and again so I could always drink something warm. She also put water in front of my door. I became more quiet, inwardly directed and connected to myself. Above all, I was very glad to be able to think about important things. Finally, I had the time.

I can still remember how suddenly, after sitting and pondering for a very long time, I heard the morning crow of the rooster and felt very happy that morning had arrived. It also gave me a very good sense about the time of day. Never before in my life had I been so happy about something like the cockle-doodle-do of a rooster. I listened with my ear pressed to the window and in my heart, there was light. Knowing that the first day was already over made me feel happy. I was also happy that it was the morning because the night has an energy that can be very frightening. Not because it's menacing, but because the night brings out dark shadows in oneself.

Later on I went back to bed and just enjoyed being there. As I was tired, I fell asleep. A few hours later, Bharati came to visit. I was very happy about this and we had some profound conversations about life and about the harmful things in our world, such as war and drug consumption. She also sang a beautiful song which raised the vibration in the room a bit more. After Bharati left the room I was back to myself with all my feelings and thoughts. This time I sat in the corner on a chair and played the OM box, which permanently emitted the primal sound of OM. I remember exactly how suddenly I started laughing at this situation. It was as if I were in a cabaret. I kept laughing louder and deeper from the heart, because I found it so funny to just just sit there and listen to this OM box. "What am I doing here?" I asked, laughing.

Minutes or hours later, I don't know exactly, I became quite tired again and went back to bed to sleep a little more. However this time, I noticed how the surrounding area became more quiet and calm. Fewer cars drove by, fewer pedestrians walked near the house. I realized it was nighttime and people had gone back to their homes. Suddenly I felt very alone. Alone and lonely. No animals, no people. Everyone for themselves. The darkness of the night also showed up in me. Fears from the past, fear of being abandoned, and also, only once, the fear of dying. As I became aware of the night and darkness in the outer world, I felt the night and darkness in myself.

After ten minutes of falling asleep, I woke up feeling satisfied. Perhaps it had been several hours later. Unfortunately I never knew, but it didn't really matter how long I had actually slept. I had been torn out of my sleep from very emotional dreams. The constant anxiety and buried emotions of everyday life appeared again and again as I slept, dreamed intensively, woke up and then slept again. Then at some point I remember that I was awake and just couldn't sleep anymore.

Suddenly it began to blink constantly in my eyes. No matter where I looked, I saw a flashing, glowing light. When I closed my eyes it was there and when I opened them, it was there. I had to put my hand over my eyes so I wouldn't get pulled out of my body, at least that's how it felt. It was impossible to sleep in this condition so I sat up and tried to meditate. That didn't work either. So I just went back to sitting there. Gradually I became very hungry and wanted something good to eat, but I had organized and planned beforehand not to eat and only drink tea. At this moment in the night and with the flashing lights, I got really hungry and started craving vegetables. Constantly I had the image in my mind of a juicy and crunchy red pepper. "Oh man!" I thought to myself.

Suddenly I heard a strange sound, as if someone were showering next door. After I had fallen asleep and then woke up again, this person was still showering. I wondered why this person was wasting so much water. At the same time, I didn't really trust my own perception because everything felt timeless. I couldn't tell the difference between one or ten minutes passing. So I let it go and just accepted this person who took long showers. Then I remember Sabine opening the door in the hallway to bring me a pot of tea. She placed the tea in front of my door and then opened the door of the next room. I heard how she had noticed that somewhere in the room water was running. It turned out that the flush valve for the toilet was out of place and the water kept running, so much that it sounded like someone was taking a shower next door.

During this time, the most pleasant thing for me was the rooster who would crow his morning song. Quickly and carefully, I went over to the window to listen to the beautiful sound. And once again the light in me turned on with all fears vanishing in no time. Everything was alive, the cars drove by, people were talking and walking. This meant it was a new day again and that really made me very happy. Interesting how you can look forward to the little things in life.

Some time later on, Bharati returned for another talk. This was always very nice for me because it allowed me to tell her what I experienced during the night. I could speak with her openly about everything with nothing to hide. To this day, I treasure that time and appreciate her very much. She was a friend who looked after me with such great care. I felt like I was in very good hands.

During our conversation I noticed the extreme flashing lights again. They became very strong especially when Bharati visited me. I told her what I was afraid of and how I felt in the night. I had also told her that I was afraid to meet someone at night that I may not get along with. Fear swept through my mind about meeting a deceased being but after our conversation, the fear disappeared. We also planned how I would leave the dark the next day and return to the light. The next morning at sunrise I would leave the room and go into nature.

The last night was very quiet and mainly characterized by the flashing lights. I had a few small fears surfacing during so-called lucid dreams, a state where one is not really asleep and not really awake. I felt like I was in a trance. This time, however, the fears felt like they were on their way out. As if they no longer had 100% control over my life. They simply became weaker.

During the last night I didn't sleep at all. I reflected on many things and thought about what I would like to do differently in the future. I also took a closer look at my friends. Which ones were good for me and those who were not. That felt very healthy.

The next morning, I heard the rooster crow again and I knew it was time. I was curious about how everything would go knowing that today was the day I would leave the darkness and return to the light. At the same time I felt internally very sad because the darkness was now very familiar and safe, like a trusted friend that I had to say goodbye to. At this moment, it was painful. Shortly after, Martin, the dear husband of Bharati, came to get me. With my eyes still covered, he guided me to a very special place. It was the first time I had looked at nature with such simplicity and attention. Observing and feeling the life and creativity, without worries and feeling completely relaxed. The trees danced and the birds sang. It was as if the light in myself was now shining brighter.

Today, a year later, I'm still bearing fruits from sowing these seeds. Overall, I've become aware of the underlying, often subconscious, mechanisms affecting my life. I see what's happening internally. It's crystal clear and I'm no longer driven by impulses. Rather, I see the impulses and decide which one I want to follow with my heart. I feel awake and alive. Through the discussions with Bharati, I've been able to understand a lot more about myself. It also led me to stop consuming various drugs. Sobriety is what I'm celebrating, a natural serenity that I was born with.

Emma from Kassel, Germany, Age 48

7-Day Individual Retreat in July 2016

I'm 48 years old, work as a teacher and love music. In the summer I travel with my partner to go paragliding in the mountains as often as possible. For many years I've studied and practiced Buddhist teachings and techniques.

My first Darkness Retreat was also my first contact with this topic and with the people at Spiritbalance. It was my first retreat in the dark. Before this, I had already spent a week alone in silence, twice.

My interest in Buddhism goes back a long time so I knew about Darkness Retreats from the traditional teachings of Tibetan Buddhism. Once I read about a yogini who went through wonderful experiences in the dark and developed incredible skills. This made a big impression on me and and for a long time I thought how it could be possible for me to experience something like this, at least to some extent. I even had plans to darken an area in my apartment, but at the same time I was concerned to do it without any outside help. By chance I found Spiritbalance's offerings on the internet. When I read there was also counseling and supervision, I knew that with their help I would finally dare to do it.

At that very moment when I first read their offer, I firmly decided to go to the Darkness Retreat. The idea of reducing all sensory impressions and above all, getting completely away from everyday life to focus only on what was going on in my head, was very appealing to me. It was my wish to give myself a good retreat and find a place where mentally, I felt well and could stay. Perhaps just being with myself would be a refuge. I imagined I could face the challenges when I felt well in such a place. I had also read about the lights. However, I got a strange feeling after reading the reports and had no desire to have these light experiences. My wish was to go on a research trip and discover things as an observer, the "I" who is always present and "intact".

I was very afraid that I had set my expectations too high and also that when I started looking into the abyss, I would suffer terrible emotions. I wasn't sure what shadows were hiding there, just waiting for the right opportunity to jump out and completely overwhelm me. My hope was to be able to withstand and have the necessary strength to go through it. My insecurity became even bigger when I thought about having to face these new situations by myself. Yet at the same time, I was incredibly inspired to figure out how to approach it. I wanted to know this! And it seemed to me that this was the best opportunity to take the leap.

Having a lot of fear coupled with even greater expectations gave me reason to do my best and prepare as much as possible. Since I have been practicing meditation regularly for years, I already had a very stable foundation. I envisioned practicing different meditations and I recorded a few meditations and mantras on a voice recorder that I took with me into the retreat. I felt that these recordings would give me inspiration and at the same time, give me the possibility to keep track of my thoughts in the dark. I also selected some yoga and tai chi exercises and practiced them beforehand so I could easily do them in the dark. I thought that the mantras, meditations, and exercises could provide some daily structure in the dark and help alleviate boredom or whatever else might arise.

Being in the dark without any distractions, my first impression was about how my own thoughts were forming, unrestricted and without interruption. I went through a lot of emotions and tapped into memories from childhood that had been lost for a long time and were emotionally upsetting.

The bamboo flute I brought with me sounded totally new. My senses, that I was still able to use, had become sharpened. My body also had a new feeling and I was fascinated by the overlapping boundaries of body and mind and at times, how the mind seemed to be completely free from the body. Dreams became clearer and thoughts calmed down in a pleasant way, not sleepy, but relaxed and attentive. Then I began experiencing light stimulus which bothered me for two days. After a while, the light calmed down and I felt my face relax. I felt at ease with whatever else might happen. I spent some time looking at the structures and forms of this light as it appeared and moved, yet couldn't be fixed to remain in place. It looked familiar and seemed like it belonged to me. I also felt very safe, more relaxed, and experienced my meditations more deeply than ever before.

When I think back to my feelings, there were times I felt bored during the Darkness Retreat and would doubt whether or not it was really a good idea to have done it. It was only after I had kept repeating all of these feelings for three days that I finally gave up trying to maintain my usual routine and just completely surrendered to the situation. From then on, it felt like a great blessing to be in the retreat. I experienced incredible sadness on the last day because I didn't want to be separated from these experiences, the closeness I felt to myself and to the new and inspiring emotions.

The counselling conversations during the first three to four days were incredibly important for me. It was very helpful for me to know that someone was watching over and observing all that was happening to me through every phase. On one level, I received explanations about the Darkness Retreat to help me understand the inner process as a physical-hormonal one. On the inner level, the conversations were very supportive to express my feelings. I also enjoyed just having a chat from time to time. In addition, the food was lovingly prepared and presented. A gentle ring of the bell signaled that there was something to eat. The caring voice that asked if everything was all right gave me the feeling of being safe. All of this helped me to sink into the darkness.

Personally, I gained greater confidence through the Darkness Retreat and also became more clear about myself. I feel more centered. Also, I look more honestly at my own mistakes and weaknesses without being scared of my flaws. Yes, I can now say that I'm able to accept myself better. My meditations have become deeper and the darkness has become my ally.

The change of my feelings, as I described above, is very reflective of the inner process I experienced in the dark. An important turning point came on the third day. My hard structured mentality calmed down and I really surrendered myself to the darkness. From this moment, the view of my inner life became clearer and the lights, who had annoyed me, became my roommates.

When I was supposed to return to the light again, I didn't want to leave because I knew that this new sense of security that I felt in myself would cease. It felt like a separation from a lover or like an involuntary birth, where I am the baby who (once again) has to come back and live another life. But when I took off the blindfold and gazed into the sunset, I was instantly reconciled with the situation. This world was so beautiful and the nature was magical and flawless. And all animals and humans moved about with dizzying speed.

Next to the tasks of everyday life such as work, house cleaning and others, my inner work and life has become more meaningful. Presently in my life, I can't imagine that I would ever want to be without meditation and contemplation. I now manage more quickly to be more centered by keeping my distance from destructive thought patterns.

I can recommend a Darkness Retreat experience to everyone, which I already did as soon as I arrived back home. But I also feel that one must really want to do it. Someone who really doesn't want to do a Darkness Retreat will probably not be harmed, but it's unlikely that they will discover something or truly learn. Whoever wants to step out of their fears, but doesn't dare, should definitely take the leap. Their courage will be rewarded.

I absolutely plan to do another Darkness Retreat! And gladly longer than 7 days. My tip to those who are interested is to give yourself a sufficiently long period of time. Because in addition to the days in the dark, it's advisable to include days before and especially afterwards. For me personally, driving faster than 50 km/h on the second day in the light was still difficult.

Philipp from Flöha, Germany, Age 32

6-Day Individual Retreat in August 2016

I'm Philipp and grew up in a small town called Flöha in Saxony. For five years I worked for a small high-tech company. Now I'm going to travel the world. This was my first retreat in the dark and it was through the internet that I found Spiritbalance. I made my decision in Spring 2016. I went to the Darkness Retreat with the desire and intention to know myself and make decisions about my life path, including leaving my job and traveling the world. To prepare for the retreat, I ate a vegan diet 2 - 3 months in advance.

Did I have any fears, concerns or insecurities? Yes and no! Yes, I was frightened because it was the first time for me to be alone in the dark for a relatively long time and I was unsure what my soul would tell me and what states of consciousness would set in. And no because I felt comfortable and would be lovingly cared for, supported and guided. I also knew that it was my decision and I was free to stop or go anytime.

During the Darkness Retreat I experienced how various life themes "emerge" and I could look at them with a new perspective. I saw my life, my parents and grandparents.

I felt a deep bond of love and connection to them. It was as if all of a sudden I could see very clearly what wonderful people stood by me all the time, giving me so much love and how it provided me with so much strength. It made me cry. Throughout my Darkness Retreat I felt hungry. I looked forward to the smoothies accompanied by the ringing bell twice a day. Eventually I noticed that this feeling in my stomach, which I thought was related to fear, was quite simply that I was hungry.

During the retreat I felt well cared for and accompanied. I could ask for as much support as I needed through the conversations and was also free to be alone with myself. In the Darkness Retreat, I took the decision to quit my current job and go on a trip around the world.

I began the Darkness Retreat feeling highly motivated to go through an inner process. I was grateful to have this time with myself. In the beginning, I structured my day somewhat with brushing my teeth, washing, doing light stretching exercises, drinking two bottles of water, etc., but after two or three days I more or less let go of this structure. I just laid in bed a lot and eventually took a shower when I needed a change. My awareness of whether I was lying awake all the time, thinking to myself, or if I was asleep and dreaming, diminished. For most of the time, I felt awake.

At the end, approximately on the fifth or sixth day, I was overcome with joy and a feeling of certainty that I had achieved what I wanted. I was clear about what I wanted for myself and my life. On the sixth night, after finding what I was inwardly searching for, I went by myself and looked out of the window at the stars until it eventually became dawn. There was a tremendous feeling of happiness and joy of knowing what action I would take for my next steps. My life has changed so much that I am now on a journey around the world. I have become more courageous and confident because I know that I have everything within myself for what I need. I can recommend a Darkness Retreat to people who feel that this method could help them find and authentically connect to themselves.

Currently I'm not planning to do another a Darkness Retreat since I'm now traveling and prefer to see what is going on outside in the world. I would like to tell you how much I truly appreciate the warmth with which I was welcomed and taken care of during my stay at Spiritbalance. A little child who sat with me the day after my Darkness Retreat at the dining table, played with two toy zebras and struck them against each other. She asked me, "Do they argue or kiss each other?" I received the answer: "They love each other." This was a moment that describes for me their lovely and wonderful way of doing things.

Maurice from Halle, Germany, Age 30

11½ -Day Individual Retreat in September 2016

Well what can I say, except that I live and learn. One day, I found out in a book about Darkness Retreats and while reading, I immediately decided that I wanted to experience this for myself. So I went, without much preparation, into my first Darkness Retreat with the intention of getting to know myself better. However, I also had my concerns. To be exact, I was afraid that I would reach my limit and wouldn't be able to go beyond it. And then the journey into the darkness began.

At first I felt good. Toward the middle of the retreat, I was terribly frightened. I went through a lot. From death, paranoia, resolving old trauma to wonderful memories of my late grandfather, everything was there. Up until the very end, I felt euphoric and full of enthusiasm. However, I wasn't used to the energy of euphoria mixed with feelings of anxiety.

Thanks to this experience in the dark, I regained my sense of basic trust and lost 10 kg, which of course made me very happy. Also my enthusiasm and drive increased after the retreat, which had been going down since 8 months.

After the retreat and going back into the light, everything was very bright. It felt unfamiliar to see it like that. However, it also felt very good to use my eyes again. After the Darkness Retreat, I realized that my thoughts about myself had changed, as well as the ways in which I was avoiding myself.

Basically, I would recommend a Darkness Retreat to many people, as it is a very good method to get to know oneself better. In my own circle of acquaintances, however, people are not so conscious and would most likely consider it crazy to do a Darkness Retreat. I definitely plan to do another Darkness Retreat. Unfortunately it won't be longer than my first since my boss didn't give me a longer holiday. But I'm firmly committed to repeat it and go deeper.

Thomas from Pfaffstätten, Austria, Age 39

10-day Silent Retreat in October 2016

I'm from Upper Austria and was born in July 1977, under the zodiac sign of Cancer with Scorpio Rising. One side of my work is as an IT manager/administrator and mechanical engineer for a large corporation that manufactures railway vehicles. On the other side, I am a human energetic worker and have my own practice for individuals and groups. I am married and the father of a wonderful son.

My spiritual path started with Kriya Yoga when I was about 19 years old, but moved into the background later on. It was reawakened when I was instructed in acting classes to trust my intuition, and the technologist in me vehemently denied such a thought. In 2016, I was a Team Leader for the Human Trust with Veit Lindau and I also took the online course "Schreibglück" (The Joy of Writing). Through this, I found Saskia John's book "Grenzerfahrung Dunkelretreat" (Darkness Retreat - Going Beyond the Limits). Something in there sounded appealing and I went on the internet. After some research, I found a Darkness Retreat in Germany. A phone call later and my decision was sealed to go through this personal experience in the dark. So it was my inner guide that ultimately led me to a 10-day retreat in complete darkness.

I'm still not sure if it was really me who chose the retreat. I mean, everything just flowed in the right direction. I had enough money, enough vacation time and the organization for my son's care went effortlessly. It was clear that this rest, time-out and experience was meant to be. In my case everything went quite spontaneously and quickly, because in only four weeks later it would be time to go.

I noticed in the months before the Darkness Retreat that I could hardly settle down. During my meditation, I simply couldn't find that space of inner peace and that tormented me even more. I wanted to find myself again and listen to my inner voice.

I also had the idea that it would be beautiful if the master plan for my future would appear during the retreat. And even if it wasn't my main objective, I thought it would be interesting to have a supernatural experience. In addition, I wanted to have a proper rest and just sleep well. After all, in recent years I had to get up several times a night to take care of my son.

I admit I had some doubts about the Darkness Retreat. I was unsure if the theme "feeling caged in" might reappear in this context. In my childhood I had traumatic experiences that referred to this theme and was concerned that I wouldn't be able to handle it. It was also the reason that I traveled by car so I could be as flexible as possible. The diet during my Darkness Retreat was based on raw food. This made me worry even more as I wasn't at all familiar with this diet. But thank God, in reality both never became an issue at all.

My preparation to go into complete darkness was very limited. I simply searched the directions to the place, got a dictaphone and downloaded some meditations and meditation music. In addition, I felt a bit insecure and had a few thoughts that it wouldn't be the right thing for me. Besides, I didn't even want to prepare. I just wanted to have my experience as direct and unfiltered as possible. For example, I didn't order the book of Saskia John. I thought to myself that I'm going to a Darkness Retreat with competent and caring professionals. I was confident that nothing would go wrong. And then came the day when I began my journey into darkness.

In the Darkness Retreat, I experienced peace, silence, confusion, extreme clarity, inner struggle, fear and oneness. Sometimes I couldn't control the rising energy. But I simply trusted that everything was right, as it was. Some meditations were incredibly enriching and I was reminded of something that Yogi Dhiranandaji recounted to me 20 years before. I saw bright golden light and heard the cosmic sound in an intensity that I could have never imagined before. Only by experiencing it first in a Darkness Retreat, could I know and feel this exhilaration.

Such spiritual experiences transcend far beyond human understanding. I can't even explain it through my own comprehension, not even poorly. Furthermore, during the time in the dark, certain jokes and word play became very funny for me. The following sayings took on a completely new meaning for me: "Wait and drink tea", "Dark Shadows", "Gossiping sounds good in the dark", "Sun salutation", "Dark thoughts" and "Festival of Lights".

During my Darkness Retreat I felt very well cared for and safe. I realized that darkness is extremely peaceful. It's not an absence of light, as I always thought, but rather the original state. To have the sun so close is like hitting the jackpot. Besides this, there was a moment when I was showering where I realized that I was truly able to really enjoy myself. This wonderful self-acceptance and self-love became more profound and meaningful for me. The darkness also taught me that my identity as Thomas is both unimportant and important.

In retrospect I can say that in the beginning, the Darkness Retreat was strange and partly confusing. For the first two days I slept and when I woke up, somehow I knew it was daytime and it wasn't true that it was dark. This was accompanied by a brief inner panic, which quickly disappeared as I remembered where I was. Then came a phase where I fully enjoyed not having to do anything. And then the part of me that wanted to change started knocking on my inner door. Through my Kriya yoga practice and the guided meditations I recorded on my dictaphone, I had tools to facilitate a fantastic personal development.

Naturally after the Darkness Retreat, it was time for me to go back to the light. That was a little weird. To be honest, I didn't imagine it being as crazy as it felt. It took a very long time, several hours, until I felt like I was back. I saw the world overflowing with abundance and felt like if I were to get involved in so many of the things it was showing to me, my system would get blown away. I also felt totally dizzy. Even now, in front of my inner eye, I can still see the magical green blades of grass. They were the first things I saw when I began opening my mask. I'll also never forget the fiery red leaves of a bush and of course, the sunset!

My time in the Darkness Retreat filled me with an inner security that I can't describe well in words. This feeling has extended into all parts of my life and is, as I said, difficult to explain. It feels as if a door has been pushed open to a whole new life. The work in my practice as a human energetic has benefited greatly. It hasn't made everything easier, I don't want to sugarcoat it, but I have reached a depth that makes me humble.

Annette from Hersbruck, Germany

3-Day Trial Retreat in October 2016

Since I'm a nature lover and like to be outdoors in nature, I went first for a weekend retreat. This introduction was done with much love. I went into the darkness by blowing out a candle light and lighting up my heart. It was surprising how I felt no hesitation or distraction to be with myself in the dark. At times, I felt wide awake with a lot of clarity. I didn't sleep so much. There were a couple moments when I could actually see in the dark. Once I recognized the white wall and another time, white tissues were clearly visible. Also the table that I didn't pay attention to on my way in, became visible. And because I had such a clear mind, I began dreaming about a very deep and dark event that I had dreamed about in a similar dream a long time before. The very fact that these perceptions and sensations appeared within such a short time during the Darkness Retreat amazed me. And now, six months after, I feel very calm and peaceful each time I think back on it. It was an intense and lasting experience. I'm very grateful to have had this, thank you.

Stefanie from Hamburg, Germany, Age 50

10-day Individual Retreat in November 2016

I'm Steffi, the mother of a 19-year-old daughter and I work as a family and children's nurse, assisting people who are dying and mourning. I am also federally certified to work as a psychotherapist. After a 3 year training in traditional medicine and shamanic practices, I gained an understanding that everything is connected beyond time and space. I am part of everything! I don't have anything to rescue nor search for any solutions. Consciousness is all around us and healing happens within us.

I had read about Darkness Retreats many years ago in a book and it left a big impression on me. After that, I spent many years searching for an offer until I found one that was suitable for my needs. When I felt the trust and confidence in the care I would receive, I made my decision. This was very important to me. I had inherited some money and could afford to do it.

My wish was to let my soul speak in the dark, to silence my ego and find out what's there. I wanted to know if the way I'm living my life is right or just a joke that I'm pretending exists otherwise.

Since I've had a strong, overall intrinsic trust for many years, I had no fears about the upcoming retreat. However, I was worried that even if I felt the need to stop, which would be ok if it happened, I would just force myself to keep on going. In preparation for the Darkness Retreat, I asked my guides from other dimensions for protection. I took my bedding and my drum into the retreat. And then it started.

During the Darkness Retreat, I was bored and had trouble finding the right words. I forgot the simplest lyrics. I was riding a mental merry-go-round and asked myself how many thoughts would fit in one minute. A lot of anger, astonishment, coldness, and pain came out in me. There was an incredible amount of light and I had past-life encounters. Again and again I received signs of trust and protection.

However, I must also say that I did not feel well in the dark. I was very cold and very bored. And there was always light everywhere. I could actually see that darkness was simply a potential for light. I just wanted to have my peace and sleep, but I wasn't tired. I hardly dreamed and could only think. It was so exhausting and annoying. The ego was always playing with me by distracting me from feeling my soul and irritating me with pain. I was angry and argued and quarreled with my ego. In my thoughts I played "Scattegories“ and asked myself questions, both big and small, receiving only partial answers. Appearing around me again and again were images and lots of light and shadow. Then all of a sudden, I was able to draw "light" letters onto objects.

My experience in the dark was annoying and I didn't know why I actually chose to do it. I was angry because Bharati wasn't there in the house for the first four days and it was only because of her that I chose not to do the retreat in nearby Lüneburg, and drove to what felt like the end of the world from Hamburg. The other two supervisors were very nice, loving and comforting, but I didn't feel safe. I wanted to cancel and leave, but spoke with Bharati before. After our conversation, I was sure that I could protect myself. Everything was fine. I told myself, "Maybe I'll never do it again so just let it go". I snarled back at my ego and could finally look at these images in peace. I saw my past lives and innumerable lost souls that were still between worlds. I wasn't frightened to see so many of these souls who wanted to go to the light because I had already had contact with the deceased before the retreat. Near the end of the retreat, I had two impressive discoveries. One, a vision of a man I'll meet and who will love, treasure and teach me something, and vice versa. That has been my wish to the universe for many years.

The last night I had a beautiful experience. It was the first time I truly FELT that I am a good person. Just as I am, with all my shadow sides. It was a realization that I don't have to do anything to be loved and that I'm free of feeling guilty. That was very touching.

During the Darkness Retreat, I also practiced the Love and Light Mantra. I directed it to people with whom I had a good relationship and also to those with whom I had broken contact. However, it was very difficult for me to concentrate. For weeks after the retreat, some of these people got in touch with me, after more than 10 years. That was amazing.

What has the Darkness Retreat done for me personally? First, I was just glad to get out of it. The rebirth during the morning leading into the day was unlike anything else, simply incredible and beautiful. Although I was moving very slowly, I went for a walk straight away on the mountain and had a smoke in the sun. Then I got in my car and drove, which I don't recommend to anyone, back to Hamburg. It was a stupid decision. I had slowed down so much that when I turned my head to look at something, it took a few seconds before I could actually see it. That's not so good when you're driving. I was frightened by everything. So my advice is to take good care of yourselves. Although in my case, no one could have stopped me from leaving. I wanted to get out of the dark and away from the smell of burning incense.

After I was back in Hamburg I was able to extend my retreat time and then around two weeks later I went into full menopause, feeling and experiencing myself very differently. The aftermaths of the retreat are incredible. I am very happy as I am and feel good about myself. I'm relaxed, calm, confidant and miles away from my impulsive reactions. The time in the dark changed me, I'm much more relaxed with myself and also with those around me. This is great. After the retreat I met the man I had seen in the vision. It was more than amazing. He looked exactly the same as he appeared in my vision. I'm reaping the fruits of my work by accepting and enjoying them.

The moment when I came back to the light after the Darkness Retreat was really like being reborn. In the morning I was taken out of the darkness, wrapped in blankets and went to watch the November sun rising up. I would have given myself more time but I felt like someone was standing next to me. It was a distraction. Then I realized it was the house cat who had come to join me. It was so nice. I also thought about how terrible it must be for babies who are born in a delivery room under neon lights.

Personally, I would only recommend a Darkness Retreat to those people who have a good basic trust, even in difficult situations, and it's a clear advantage if one can meditate.

Hans-Uwe from Hainichen, Germany, Age 60

10-day Individual Retreat in December 2016

I was married for 28 years and have four children. Triggered by different experiences, I fell into a spiral from childhood that I couldn't get out of. I went to two psychologists but unfortunately, the sessions did not give the desired result.

My Darkness Retreat in December 2016 with Bharati and Martin was my first experience in a Darkness Retreat. My idea was to get out of the endless loop of my childhood and work through my past.

In preparation for my Darkness Retreat, I spent a day at home in a dark room to see if I was afraid in the dark. I realized that I wasn't afraid and went ahead and made an appointment with Bharati.

Being very open to new things, I was curious about all that awaited me. In the first three days during the conversations, I spoke about everything that was burdening me. The first evening I saw a dim strand of light and then images, which I couldn't recognize as they changed very quickly. On the second night I saw a light, shining as strong as a light bulb. Bharati told me that it was the Divine Light. The tinnitus in my ear had increased and I suspected it was due to everything I was speaking about. On the third night I had a strong earache and couldn't sleep. The following day, I continued my conversation with Martin and he showed me a technique to feel better about myself. He also showed me how I could get rid of the past spiral. It still works today. In the dark, I had a memory of an operation during my childhood. Martin put me in a trance and I saw images from the past century. Afterwards he told me these images, which I had never seen or experienced before, had come from a past life.

Bharati explained that within these ten days, one can lose their sense of time. Unfortunately this was not the case with me. At times I felt bored and on the sixth day, I was freezing cold. On the seventh day I wanted to stop the Darkness Retreat. But after speaking with Bharati, I learned that just before an emotional breakthrough the body attempts to fight against it. I did some relaxation exercises and then decided I would stay in the dark. Unfortunately, the tinnitus prevented me from going deeper inside. Personally, the Darkness Retreat helped me to process my memories of the past. I also see colors much more vividly than before.

The moment I "went to the light" again took place in the early morning just before sunrise. I was led outside to a chair on the terrace, wrapped in blankets and given hot tea to drink. I began slightly lifting my eye mask so that some light came to my eyes, which were still closed. Then, while keeping my eyes closed, I took off the eye mask. I began blinking until I could open my eyes completely. The view of the valley below was wonderful. A veil of mist floated and covered the surrounding area.

A change that happened after the Darkness Retreat, in both my life and for me personally, is that I see life no longer as a burden, but as a gift from nature. My self-awareness is also more stable and balanced.

For those who are interested, I encourage them to watch the videos from Bharati and Spiritbalance on YouTube. If it sparks an inner desire or further supports an idea you have, then I would recommend to participate in a Darkness Retreat. I currently have no concrete plans to do another Darkness Retreat. At the moment I'm interested in family constellation, which goes very well for me. However I have thought about the idea of doing another Darkness Retreat.

Manuel from Röllbach, Germany, Age 34

12-day Individual Retreat in December 2016

I work as a software developer. Since a long time, I've been interested in various themes related to consciousness. My interest was on and off until about one or two years ago when I became very interested again. It could have been triggered through reaching high states of consciousness during meditation and which are still present in me. I wanted to learn and try new methods so I enrolled in various courses and seminars. Among them were various yoga teachings, seminars on Christian mysticism, Zen Buddhism, silent meditation retreats and a few others.

It was during a mystical teaching seminar that I learned about the possibility of doing a Darkness Retreat. The seminar leader brought up the subject of a Darkness Retreat and explained that it can also act as a kind of spiritual accelerator. He compared the Darkness Retreat to an express train that quickly takes its passengers into the deep hidden side of their nature. I was totally fascinated by it, so much that I decided it would be necessary for me to try at some point. It was during that first introduction at the seminar that I made my decision. Then, of course, I wanted more information and began researching the topic which only increased my fascination. A few weeks later I called Sasbachwalden and booked my retreat.

I imagined that in contrast to a normal retreat, the reduction and withdrawal from daily stimuli would allow easier and better access to my heart. My idea was to deepen and accelerate my practice through the retreat. Of course I also hoped to experience something really extraordinary such as astral travel, but it wasn't my main focus. I didn't have any fears or concerns and didn't do anything specific to prepare myself for the Darkness Retreat. Moreso, I just learned a lot of methods and practices that I could do during the retreat. Something that would give me confidence, just in case "the roof came tumbling down" in the dark.

During the first days I slept a lot. In between sleeping, I always meditated. In contrast to my previous sitting meditation practice, I mediated a lot while lying down. Since I had been sleeping a lot, I could remain awake and concentrate well. First thing, I would take an early shower, which was no problem in the dark, and then I practiced some yoga exercises to get my circulation going. That worked surprisingly well. Before I started my yoga practice, I carefully checked that all the walls were far away before placing my yoga mat on the floor. Afterwards, I slowly sipped a delicious smoothie for my breakfast. Then I switched from meditating to sleeping to sitting in the chair to thinking and so on.

Once a day there was time to meet and have a private conversation. These were very helpful for me. I could discuss everything that was going through my head. I also found it good that the counsellors for the conversation changed. That was good for me because it's normally the case that everyone in an ashram has a slightly different focus or different strengths. So I could talk about my experiences and difficulties on one day and during another day, I was guided by someone through a meditation or learned something about diet, meditation and health.

During the first days my thoughts overwhelmed me. It was very hard to concentrate because of the endless, useless everyday thoughts circulating in my head. I felt that I was almost on the edge of going crazy. Almost. With time the thoughts reduced and helped my meditation become quieter and deeper. Somehow, from the moment my thoughts became quieter, my body became more sensitive and open. I noticed this particularly when I was lying down in meditation. I was physically more relaxed than in a seated meditation. Sometimes it would feel like the body was vibrating a little. It was a good feeling.

After a few days, I had a lucid dream. I became aware that this dreamworld was "in the light" yet I wanted to stay in the dark for the few remaining days. This seemed strange and I took it as just a dream. I feel that darkness can be a very helpful for conscious dreaming. In total, during the whole retreat, I had two lucid dreams. That is already a very good amount for me.

After some days, I joined a group meeting instead of the individual meeting. I enjoyed this very much. All of the participants introduced themselves followed by mantra singing, recounting interesting and informative experiences, sharing wisdom and much more. In addition, I gained insight into the experiences of other participants.

During the first few days I was really annoyed by my thoughts. They were constantly in front of me and it was draining my energy without bringing any benefit. I noticed this especially when I had sunken into a deep meditation and was no longer involved in thinking, only being. These moments of clarity were fantastic. It didn't matter at all where I was, I could have been on a beach in the Bahamas or sitting in my darkroom, it was this feeling of being present that was so wonderful. The time passed quite quickly during the few remaining days of the retreat. During the last few days I was struggling a bit due to feeling restless. One day, I heard the sound of a snowball fight and someone stomping through the snow. It made me want to go outdoors. To calm down my go-getter attitude, I went for a sound massage. That also worked well.

Then something a bit special happened. Immediately after the Darkness Retreat I got sick and had to go to the nearest hospital for a while. Even during that time, I could really count on the Spiritbalance team for their care and support. We talked to each other on a daily basis, they brought all of my personal belongings to me, visited me, cheered me up when I felt a little bit knocked down, even scraped the ice from my car and so much more. Everyone took care of me as a matter of course. At times it left me speechless.

The retreat really did seem to be a type of spiritual accelerator. A lot of what I experienced was more intense than usual, which is probably due to the darkness. I didn't have any major, extraordinary spiritual experience, but everything I did experience helped me grow. Simply put, it was a big step forward.

Now, a few months after the retreat, I can sink into meditation much easier and deeper than was the case a while back. I also feel much more relaxed and calm in my everyday life.

It's difficult to write about and describe my internal process during Darkness Retreat. Primarily, my thoughts were strongly in the forefront. Thoughts that are most likely present during my everyday life but had been hidden. During the retreat time, I tried to deal with those thoughts by processing and getting rid of them which felt really liberating when it actually happened. I also learned to give up control and quit trying so hard to make everything perfect. I realized that it was only me who was pressuring myself to behave like this. This theme came up again shortly after the retreat when I went to the hospital and thus had to release all control. It was a process that continued well beyond the end of the retreat. Currently there is so much in me that has changed, I can't really describe all of it. It any case, it goes in a positive direction even if it doesn't always appear to be.

It was in the afternoon that I returned back "into the light". Everything was covered in snow and I had an incredible view of the valley. But my eyes were not accustomed to the brightness and it made me somewhat dizzy. So I stayed in the house where the light was not so bright and looked out the window. I sat for a while and marveled at the surroundings which looked as if it had come straight out of a fairy tale.

I would recommend a Darkness Retreat to people who already have a spiritual practice because for me, I feel it would have been very difficult without mine. But in general, I recommend it to anyone who feels attracted to it. As I recently completed my Darkness Retreat, I'm not planning to do another one at the moment. For the time being, I'm continuing my practice in the light.

Gabriela from Stäfa, Switzerland, Age 56

8-Day Individual Retreat in January 2017

In early 2017, I went for a short 8-day Darkness Retreat. As soon as I heard about it I felt a strong resonance and signed up very spontaneously. I had no fears and have never felt uncomfortable in the dark. There was something magical that attracted me

Experiencing the joy, inner peace, gratitude and feeling of just being present surpassed anything I could have imagined. It was simply an incredible and amazing experience.

After arriving home and a few days back into my everyday life, I could easily feel that I experienced a positive change. It was very enriching for me yet I know that I need to keep my meditation practice consistent to sustain the positive effects.

In a few days I'm getting married and feel very grateful for this new opening in myself.

Klara from Sasbachwalden, Germany, Age 29

10-Day Individual Retreat in February 2017

At the very beginning when I met Bharati and Martin and learned about the very high spiritual experiences that become possible during a Darkness Retreat, I knew immediately that I would dive into the darkness as soon as possible. In February 2017 it was finally time and the gate opened for me to go into a 10-Day Darkness Retreat.

In preparation for the retreat and in general, I lead a healthy lifestyle and have a regular sadhana (spiritual practice). In retrospect, this practice helped me very much during my time in the dark. In advance, I made a list and wrote down thoughts about what was important for me in the retreat. I decided to take my guitar, yoga mat and writing instruments. I'm a person who has always been afraid of the dark and had doubts as to whether I could make my way through it and come out alive. So I made a firm decision that I would face my fears and grow beyond them. I really wanted to feel peace within myself.

My journey into the dark began as soon as the light went out. It was the total opposite of my preconceived anxiety. Everything was quiet and I had the space and time to feel comfortable and relax right away. During the next days I went through very different situations and processes. There were days when I was deep within myself, connected with the Divine and feeling very peaceful. On other days I was completely displaced and went through some deep processes that gave me a lot of clarity. Sometimes I got caught up in a film of my own thoughts and couldn't get out of it. This is where the daily conversations really helped me.

During the last days of my retreat we celebrated Shivaratri, the Hindu festival celebrating Shiva and his marriage to Parvati. The whole day had been difficult and I really felt like I had reached one of the most difficult points. It was very black, not only around me but also inside me. I could barely endure this feeling of inner tension and anger. I was on my knees. Then, on this full moon evening, I decided to bathe myself in ashes. I rubbed myself with holy ashes from top to bottom. I had never done this before and didn't really know what to expect. But I really felt on the verge of despair and I thought to myself "Ok, I'm just going to do it and try to sleep". I couldn't think of anything better. The next morning I woke from sleeping feeling fresh and free. I felt so peaceful and clear. On this day I preferred to remain in silence. I felt that Shiva was very close to me along with the power that unfolded in me the night before.

Since I had never had a "light experience", for example, seeing an angel or shining lights, on this day I made a very clear announcement to the universe, "I want an experience, however it is, I just want one!" It was like a real, proper demand. And then rather unexpectedly, I took off on an astral journey. It was so incredibly real. This experience showed me on a very deep level how my mind was working. It was like a dog chasing his tail. At first I would become totally absorbed in it by searching and running after things to find out where my "mistakes" were. I also saw how I was chasing and could then pull myself away from it. I looked objectively at situations that were happening on the outside to see them as they really existed. Time and again I ran in circles and busied myself with thoughts. I recognized the fake conditioning of my mind. This was a deep and impressive experience.

And on my last day, as if I really needed to have it confirmed once and for all, I had to face my fears in a dream. It was the moment when I felt the most fear, but I was able to go through it. I didn't mind going back "to the light". To this day I still feel how much strength it gave me. Now I feel much more free and confident to face my fears.

Despite the challenges I mentioned, I felt very well throughout the Darkness Retreat. The "nothingness" gave me so much space to be and allowed me to rest completely. I've never been so relaxed. It is really a privilege to be able to escape all the external stimuli and dive deep into oneself. Of course I wasn't always relaxed and calm. But nevertheless, in the darkness I was always led back into a quiet room. In the dark you have to move slowly and carefully because if you don't, you'll hurt yourself over and over from bumping into objects and obstacles.

The daily conversations with my Darkness Retreat counsellor helped me to move through my process and inspired me to try out new meditation techniques. I felt, and still feel, a deep connection and security within myself. It's like I dropped an anchor to hold me close and stay connected to my inner core. Regardless of any external circumstances, I feel more calm and relaxed. After this experience, the fears lost much of their power over me and I've become stronger. The first rays of light after the retreat were stunningly beautiful. It was a blessing to once again, stand under the open sky. To see the world again was like seeing it for the first time. Not because the world had changed, but because I felt very different in myself. Since the Darkness Retreat many things in my life and inside of me have changed. This is mainly due to the fact that now I'm able to access my inner self and relax more easily. Some of the relationships with certain members of my family progressed and improved. I see life with different eyes and feel more in touch with myself. My inner space is more accessible and balanced which helps me to deal with all of life's changes.

I can recommend to everyone to make time and take the steps to go through a Darkness Retreat. This experience is as valuable as opening your eyes. In the darkness we can get fully in touch with ourselves and totally relax. It gives us clarity and a better understanding of ourselves and our life. Unlike a wellness therapy or taking a holiday, it is a fundamentally life-changing experience that is both relaxing and lasting. Above all, it's for people interested in self-inquiry. It gives the possibility for one to ask essential questions about life and themselves. I'm sure that they won't be disappointed when they surrender to the darkness and ask for answers. When I'm able, I would definitely like to go back to the darkness for another retreat.

Kurt from Kreuzlingen, Germany

10-Day Individual Retreat

Over the past 10 years, I've traveled regularly to India to attend a spiritual university and experience powerful spiritual teachings. At the center of all these experiences is the mantra, "Om Sat Chit Ananda" (I am truth, I am consciousness, I am bliss). This mantra is the Sanskrit response to the question, "Who am I?" I've chanted it thousands of times without really feeling and experiencing what it means. This was my starting point when I heard a lecture by Saskia John about her experiences in a Darkness Retreat in Germany. Until then, I thought it was only in Asian countries with Buddhist or Hindu culture where people practiced retreating into dark caves to deepen their spiritual experience.

I was immediately fascinated by the incredible possibilities she recounted. For me, the most surprising thing was the fact that in the dark, "spontaneous" healing often occurred. Then I found out that Bharati (a good friend of mine from my ashram days in India) was offering the perfect conditions for a Darkness Retreat in the beautiful Black Forest and I immediately booked a 10-day retreat as soon it became possible.

I didn't do anything consciously to inform myself about other experiences in the dark. I wanted to go into the process spontaneously and without any expectations. For the first two to three days I slept for a long time. While awake I enjoyed lying in the warm bed and observing my thoughts without any distraction. For the very first time I felt the meaning of the mantra, "I am truth, I am consciousness, I am bliss".

"I am truth". My body worked perfectly without any effort, just simply being present as I was in the dark. Besides the two litres of tea that I drank everyday, my body didn't need anything. After about 6 days, any remaining tension was gone and I felt totally in sync with nature, just like animals and plants which are also in a state of "being". This experience freed me of any of my normal, constant concerns about my body. I felt that my body knows what's best for itself and my mind doesn't have to worry about it. I can simply enjoy it as a beautiful vehicle that allows me to participate in life on this planet.

"I am consciousness". In the dark where one doesn't see any physical limitation, I suddenly and very clearly realized that I am not limited to my body. I could playfully expand myself to fill the whole room, the whole ashram, and even to the sky. This expansion of consciousness and being able to move far beyond the limitations of the physical body and the dark room brought a beautiful clarity of what it means to be connected with everything and ultimately with the cosmos. My feelings of loneliness

and abandonment were miraculously healed. This new freedom enabled me to search for my "higher self" and showed me something totally unexpected.

"I am bliss". I could easily get in touch with Mother Mary. An intense feeling of happiness flowed through me when she appeared before me in her radiant beauty. For the first time, I felt bliss. This door was closed in my normal "seeing" state. In the darkness this experience was simply given to me. And every time when I joined in Divine Union with Mother Mary, she presented me with this enormous gift.

In addition to these experiences, the darkness brought even more surprises. I could perceive the colors of chakras projected into the room. At first they were blurry but then became clear. Fortunately, the dominant color was green from the heart chakra. Also the room was never completely dark. It appeared dim, like a lunar landscape. The room became more visible and I believe this was due to the third eye becoming more alert and open. I suddenly realized that our ancestors, who lived in dark caves, could find their way around without fire.

From Day 5, my sensory channels and perception became so open that I saw beings from other dimensions. It was during times like this that I felt extremely lucky to have had Bharti's guidance in the daily conversations to understand and make sense of these apparitions.

A special experience was when I returned back to the light. Seated on the terrace before sunrise, I took off my blindfold. The view looked over and across the Rhine Valley, which was covered in fog. Seeing the sky, clouds, surrounding nature and feeling the first drops of rain was overwhelming. The rising sunlight flowed through me with the deepest gratitude and continues to flow this day. The strong and elevated sense of perception gave me such clarity to acknowledge the great gift we are given of being able to see the world. Greeting me with this beautiful gift of seeing the world with open eyes was a beautiful rainbow forming in the sky. It's no exaggeration that these few minutes have left the deepest impression in my consciousness. The beauty of creation is unsurpassed when we are truly able to see it.

In summary, I can say that it takes courage to go into a Darkness Retreat for a certain period of time. However, the darkness holds gifts for us, individually selected and just right for each person.

Darkness Retreat in the Black Forest

As we manage to let go of our surroundings, we stop projecting ourselves onto the outside world and literally begin to look within. This way, it is possible to transform the Ego-Experience into simply 'being', which brings with it a wonderful sense of unity and 'having arrived'.

We invite you to have a cost-free introductory consultation with one of our Darkness Retreat supervisors via telephone or Skype to discuss and clarify any questions and wishes.

- What do you expect from your Darkness Retreat?
- Would you like to do an individual retreat or be part of a group?
- What length would be best for you?
- Would you like to do it in silence or be supported on a daily basis with a counsellor?

To discuss all other questions, concerns and wishes for a personalized Darkness Retreat, call us at **+49 7841-8392417** and arrange your personal consultation with a Darkness Retreat counsellor. You can find more information about the procedure, the premises and our team of counsellors at: **www.darknessretreat.net**

Darkness Retreat Training

The Darkness Retreat is a powerful tool for inner transformation. Free from religion and dogma, its place in the world is to heal our soul, give us the clarity and strength to accomplish our life tasks with joy.

To accompany this intensive process, open and genuine counsellors are needed to listen, help the client explore their inner process and encourage them to get to the deepest part of their individual experience. This is the reason that in 2016, Bharati and Martin began sharing their knowledge for the first time to train a group of Dark Retreat supervisors and counsellors. There is now such a big demand for Darkness Retreats that we need more support!

The aim of the Darkness Retreat Supervisor/Counsellor Training is to convey the knowledge and skills necessary to independently organise and supervise Darkness Retreats which conform to our high quality standards. Special attention is given to teaching the core essentials of psychology, as well as imparting spiritual knowledge.

The training for the Darkness Retreat Supervisor/ Counsellor is comprised of three phases:

- **Phase 1:** Acquisition of important basic knowledge and personal Darkness Retreat experience
- **Phase 2:** Gaining experience in client counseling, deepening of existing knowledge
- **Phase 3:** Intensive self-reflection and acquisition of in-depth knowledge about energetic healing processes

Successful completion of Phase 1 enables trainees to carry out Darkness Retreats under supervision. Phase 2 empowers them to independently carry out and supervise their own Darkness Retreats.

Would you like to become a supervisor and counsellor to help guide people through their Darkness Retreat experience?

Call us at **+49 7841-8392417** and arrange a personal phone call with Bharati and Martin.

You can find more information about the training, prices and dates at: **www.darknessretreat.net/training/**

Notes

Zeitfracht Medien GmbH
Ferdinand Jühlke Straße 7
99095 Erfurt, Deutschland
produktsicherheit@kolibri360.de